June 25,

To Vicki,

A cherished member of
Barle-Rose Wohlstetter family.

With love & affection,

Johnny

THE RIGHT TIME
THE RIGHT PLACE

THE RIGHT TIME
THE RIGHT PLACE

CHARLES WOHLSTETTER

FOREWORD BY STEVE FORBES

APPLAUSE
NEW YORK • LONDON

AN APPLAUSE ORIGINAL
The Right Time, The Right Place
by Charles Wohlstetter
Copyright © 1997 the Estate of Charles Wohlstetter

Library of Congress Cataloging-in-Publication Data

Library of Congress catalog card number: 97-80380

British Library Cataloging-in-Publication Data

A catalogue copy of this book is available from the British Library

APPLAUSE BOOKS

211 West 71st Street
New York, NY 10023
Phone (212) 496-7511
Fax: (212) 721-2856

A&C BLACK

Howard Road, Eaton Socon
Huntington, Cambs PE19 3EZ
Phone 0171-242 0946
Fax 0171-831 8478

Distributed in the U.K. and European Union by A&C Black

Table of Contents

FOREWORD

STEVE FORBES

The life story of Charles Wohlstetter was of a kind that would have thrilled Abraham Lincoln. From a humble background, he emerged as one of the most successful, forceful entrepreneurs of this century. Starting at a young age on Wall Street, he became a prosperous stockbroker (he foresaw the 1929 Crash but was unable to convince his skeptical employer of it; he subsequently started his own firm). In 1961, he launched an independent telephone company that was sold thirty years later to GTE for $6.6 billion.

It has become a cliche to describe a multi-faceted individual as a "Renaissance man." Too bad. Wohlstetter's range of interests was breathtaking. He was a screenwriter, viniculturist and philanthropist. He had a brilliant grasp of politics, recognizing before most others the dead-end of modern liberal statism. He was a supply-sider before that term was invented. He had deep and wide-ranging knowledge of medicine and music. The only activity he didn't master to his taste was that proverbial stumbling block, golf.

The man was remarkably free of that bane of human nature, envy. Perhaps he and his brother Albert fought each other as youngsters. But there was no sibling rivalry in Charles' enormous pride in his brother. Albert, of course, virtually created our nuclear weapons doctrine that made credible our policy of

Charles & Malcolm Forbes, *The Highlander*

containment, which won us the cold war and shattered the Soviet Empire. Charles was always sending out pieces by or about his brother. An exuberant man, Charles couldn't understand Albert's self-effacement and did everything he could to promote him and his extraordinarily insightful views.

The man was never afraid of controversy, of going against the grain. When a few years ago it became fashionable for large, public sector pension funds to start telling corporate management how to run their business, Charles was appalled. In effect, he asked, What did they know? He never minded having his performance measured and judged, but he couldn't stand the idea of brickbats being thrown by political types who had no understanding of what entrepeneurship and managing a competitive enterprise was all about. He raised a valid point concerning those pension funds: Who gave these political appointees their authority? Were they elected by their fund's beneficiaries? Did they consult with these beneficiaries before taking a course of action? This forceful man always believed in accountability.

Charles Wohlstetter was one of those dynamos who exuded energy, ideas and a zest for life.

S. F.

1

BEGINNINGS

Like many an author, I have spent a great deal of time attempting to compose a suitably impressive opening sentence. After the usual amount of staring into space or tossing painfully inadequate efforts into the waste basket, I succumbed to the temptation to refer back to the Classics, to reread the great literary beginnings for inspiration. Down off the shelf came Cervantes, Jane Austen, and Herman Melville in hope that some of their magic might rub off on me. I can confidently assert that none of it has. Allow me, then, just to begin.

I was born not in a little village of La Mancha whose name I don't care to remember, but in the New York City of 1910. My grandparents, enterprising, cosmopolitan, Jewish, left the Austro-Hungarian empire in the latter half of the last century in the wave of immigrants that included the Bloomingdales, the Lehmans, and the Strausses, all of whom came to this country not to escape persecution, but to find a better way of life. My father Philip, born twenty years after their arrival, graduated from

City College just before the turn of the century; shortly thereafter, he married my mother Nellie who bore him four children:
my brothers Bill and Albert; my sister Helene; and myself. My
birth certificate lists me as "Carl Henry Wohlstetter," but everyone called me Charles or Charlie. (This, by the way, was another
one of my potential beginning sentences; but since you, the
reader, are a perfect stranger, I didn't feel comfortable grabbing
you by the collar, so to speak, by opening with, "Call me Charlie.")

Father went on to become the chief counsel for the Metropolitan Opera Company in its glory days. We entertained the
legendary Enrico Caruso, the diva Galli-Curci, and the popular
tenor Milo Pico. Even maestro Gatti Cassaza dined at our
board, as did Merola, the conductor of the San Francisco Symphony. Spirescu, the Romanian conductor at the Met, was also
a regular. Dad started one of the original phonograph companies in America, the Rex Talking Machine Company, with
Caruso and other operatic greats under contract. How well I remember the wind-up Victrola which played the recordings on
thick scratchy vinyl of those marvelous performers. What a far
cry from today's sound-perfect compact discs.

My father was never given the opportunities to capitalize on
the originality of his venture. His promising enterprise became
a casualty of the First World War. The factory in Wilmington,
Delaware, was coveted by the DuPonts, who wanted it to crank
out armaments that would teach the Germans not to fool
around with us. With a Teutonic name like Wohlstetter, poor
Dad didn't stand a chance in the debate. His charm apparently
eluded both the government and the DuPonts. We Yanks were
going to hammer the Hun and save the world for democracy.
Whether or not we ultimately did (and I have to register my
doubts), my family ended up losing its worldly possessions.

My father died of a heart attack in 1918 when I was just

eight; he was forty-nine years old. I can only speculate on what impact the loss of his visionary investment had on his demise. I didn't realize until years later what a great invention my father had; it was close to the prototypes of the radio and the television. Anyway, what the hell did the DuPonts know about music?

I have memories of Dad seated by the window, deep in thought, but most of what I know of him has been pieced together from the accounts of others. My brother Albert, four years my junior, claims to have clear recollections of him, and regales me from time to time with early childhood memories. He recalls Dad as a dandy dresser, fond of fine wines. Ordinarily, I would scowl and leave the room if anyone proposed anything so patently nonsensical, but my brother is not just anyone. When he claims to remember the design on the legs of our dining-room table, I just nod my head, since I have learned not to argue with my younger sibling. Moreover, had President Bush listened more closely when Albert was on the President's Foreign Intelligence Advisory Board (PFIAB), or read Albert's studies on Iraq, issued when he co-chaired the Defense Policy Council, Bush might not have been evicted from 1600 Pennsylvania Avenue to be numbered among the unemployed.

The remainder of my family, as I've mentioned, consisted of an older sister, Helene, and an older brother, Bill. After my father's demise, Bill, carrying the full weight of his fifteen years, became the male head of the family. He was truly our anchor. Forced to leave school in order to help support the family, he sacrificed his career. Bill had a wonderful sense of humor, and grew to be a man of extraordinary diligence and character. He was so bright that I have often wondered what he would have achieved with the benefit of schooling. Many was the time, as a young man, that he gave me financial assistance, for which I can never remember him demanding repayment. But that was how our family operated; we were there for each other at all times, regardless of the circumstances.

After Dad's death, my mother, Nellie, was left to care for four growing children on a very small income. Dad's vision of the future didn't include insurance. Mother somehow managed by selling imported Parisian lingerie to friends and relatives. I have painful recollections of her toting a battered straw suitcase from door to door, and steadfastly refusing my offers to carry it. If I was playing ball with friends, I would throw down my glove and try to wrest the bag from her grasp. "No, Charles," she would say. "You go back and play with your friends." I would often cry myself to sleep at night in frustration at our situation.

We lived in a newly-constructed apartment building up on 162nd Street in Washington Heights. 75 Fort Washington Avenue, with its six stories and iron-gated entrance, was a skyscraper to me. At the time, the subway only ran to 145th Street. The city was in the process of extending it through to 181st Street, but work was still at a very early stage. From our rear windows we could see the small hills and grassy land that ran directly to the North Hudson River just past the New York Central Railroad tracks. Not a single house blocked our view. Today, this whole area is part of the Barrio.

North of 165th Street was really "country." There were farms, even an occasional cow. At around 165th Street and Fort Washington Avenue, running down toward the Hudson River, was the New York Institution for the Deaf, which was widely known, in those days before political correctness, as the "Dummy Institution." There was a steep hill outside the fence.

Automobiles had not yet taken over the world, and the street was virtually bare of traffic. During a period of snow, the "Dummy Hill" was our own version of the Swiss Alps, and we would leap onto our Flexible Flyers and zoom down the hill at what seemed like rocket speed without traffic there to stop us. Environmental doom-sayers might claim that recent winters are getting colder because of holes in the ozone layer, but I can confidently assert that when I grew up we had snow in New York before Thanksgiving. We would build snow forts on street corners and fire snowballs at one another, with frozen ears, ruddy cheeks, and wet wool gloves.

In my neighborhood, there were formal seasons in sports as rigid as any we have today. In September, after school had started, we played our version of football in a small, rock-strewn park, the Greenies, overlooking the Hudson River. It wasn't much of a park. Grass was sparse and there were plenty of sharp stones to tear into stockings and pants. Our football teams were generally five or six to a side. We made up for our lack of num-bers by our enthusiasm and willingness, both before and after the ball was snapped, to knock an opponent to the ground. Winter was ice-skating and sleigh-riding time, and with the ar-rival of spring, everything but baseball (and the versions of it played in the street, called "stickball" or "punchball") was put out of mind. The sound of shattering glass frequently rent the air as balls propelled by a broomstick made contact with a neighbor's window. This would attract the threatening atten-tion of the cop on the beat, a burly Irishman named Parsons, who would survey the damage with distaste and, waving his nightstick in the air, bellow in a broad Irish accent, "Beat it, or I'll wrap me shillelagh around your neck." Invariably, by this time, a safe distance away, we would serenade him with our ver-sion of heroic verse, "Brass buttons, blue coat/couldn't catch a nanny goat."

Summertime was something else. Come evening, after an early dinner, we would congregate on the street and either play games like Red Rover, Prisoner's Base, and Johnny Ride a Pony or compete in short-distance foot races against another neighborhood, matching our fleetest and skinniest kids against the best of theirs. Sometimes we would even arrange fistfights between their neighborhood champion and our most favored warrior, Michael Lepore, the son of the local iceman. In those days, ice was delivered in a truck drawn by one or two horses, and we would jump on in back and chip off pieces. Michael, a quiet, not at all rambunctious kid, had nevertheless built himself into a formidable muscle man by helping his father swing twenty-five and fifty pound blocks of ice up onto the cart with a pair of tongs. Forty years later, sometime in the late fifties, my older brother's wife had a rather nasty intestinal disorder and was referred to a Park Avenue specialist, a Dr. Michael Lepore, whose first words to her were, "So, how is Charles?"

I attended P.S. 46 at 155th Street and St. Nicholas Avenue. It was not far from the Polo Grounds, and, as I grew up, it was possible for me to leave school at three from time to time and sit on Coogan's Bluff and watch the baseball game. There was not so much inside stuff between manager and players in those days, so that the game finished in reasonable time. I could still be home in time to do homework or deliver packages for the local tailor. This job was my first lesson in risk and reward. It had its dangerous side — the necessity of frequently crossing the turf of the tough Amsterdam Avenue kids — but it also had one glorious upside: among the tailor's customers were Babe Ruth and Giant's first baseman George Kelly, both of them big tippers and generous sources of free tickets.

Occasionally, after school, I took part in plays produced by a little theater group at the YMHA. That ensemble boasted the likes of Paul Stewart and Everett Sloane, future members of the

Mercury Theatre. Even at that young age of twelve or fourteen they were talking about the stage as a career; for me, it was just good fun, a way to stay off the streets. It was our version of playing ball or watching television. Some of my other boyhood friends grew up to be famous theater figures: Abe Burrows, who co-wrote the book to *Guys and Dolls*; Frank Loesser, who wrote *The Most Happy Fella*; Burton Lane, the composer who found his crock of gold at the end of *Finian's Rainbow*; and Jerry Chodorov, who co-authored *My Sister Eileen* with Joseph Fields.

On Saturdays. some of us would trudge downtown to Joe Leblang's ticket office in the basement of Gray's drugstore on Broadway. A half-hour before curtain time, theater box offices sent their unsold seats to Leblang's, where they could be purchased at a fraction of their face price. When I was twelve years old, I saw John Barrymore's Hamlet for fifty-five cents. I saw the *Ziegfeld Follies* for seventy-five. I was never in the fourth row on the aisle, but my young eyes and ears took it all in. The 1920s presented a theatrical bounty that, in all likelihood, had never occurred before and which will probably never be known again. Raymond Massey, Alfred Lunt and Lynn Fontanne, Edward G. Robinson, Walter Hampton, Helen Hayes, and countless other stars all held me in thrall in one play after another as they trod the boards in the theater center of the world. At the final curtain I left the theater and walked home on air, often repeating certain lines that had struck me as memorable.

I loved the movies too, of course, and my brother Bill, who was an usher at the Costello cinema, would sneak me in at the side door. There I would thrill to the long-running *Perils of Pauline* starring the lovely Pearl White. An episode was once filmed on the roof of our apartment building, and there I was, seeing it on the silver screen. My friend Milton Berle appeared as a juvenile in another episode. But the stage was my first love; to it I returned again and again, like a devoted suitor.

I got to know a fellow who ran the soda pop concession in some of the theaters, and I landed a job selling lemonade at the back of the house. Thus it was that I saw Donald MacDonald (who appeared in such stirring melodramas as *Beware of Widows*), Earle Larimore (co-starring in the historical drama *Juarez and Maximilian* with Edward G. Robinson), and many others for free. It was common knowledge, even to those of us who sold pop, that the Theater Guild did not share our great estimation of Alfred Lunt and Lynn Fontanne. The Guild argued strenuously that the husband-and-wife team should not appear on stage together in *The Guardsman*, but in 1924 the play was a huge hit at the Garrick Theater, and was even filmed as an early "talkie." Broadway glittered in those days. The Times Square area boasted seventy-five theaters in 1927, and an astonishing two hundred and sixty-eight plays opened that year. (Today there are thirty-five theaters, and thirty-seven plays opened in 1994.) It was not unusual to see Helen Hayes or Leslie Howard open two plays in a single year. Interestingly, thirty percent of them were either great successes or at least minor hits.

From my early days in Washington Heights until my late teens, when we moved down to 110th Street in exchange for a two months' rent concession, our family teetered on the edge of financial disaster but always found ways to keep its spirits high and its feet out of its collective mouth. Dinners were especially memorable and often consumed two-and-a-half hours: the conversation was lively and in some ways theatrical, but never truculent, which confounded some of our unsuspecting guests but amused us mightily. Though Albert, our undisputed ringmaster, tolerated no popular magazines in the house and instantly vaporized any errant copies of *The Saturday Evening Post* or *Argosy*

All-Star Weekly, he was perfectly willing to examine any topic under the sun provided the discussion transcended the mere stating of opinions, and was pursued with rigor and intellectual accuracy. Even as simple a topic as Babe Ruth's batting average would be challenged and qualified from the start unless one had adequately prepared for sharp interrogation. I still remember the time my best friend, Sylvan Coleman, who later went on to become President of E. F. Hutton, innocently announced that he had just seen a new play, *It Is a Wise Child*. The title of this David Belasco comedy referred to some recent scandal revealing the illegitimacy of a movie star's offspring. Sylvan casually remarked, "'It is a wise child that knows his own father.' Shakespeare." "Wrong!" was the outraged chorus at our table. "Act II of *The Merchant of Venice*, Launcelot Gobbo: 'It is a wise father that knows his own child.'" Even now, I find myself looking back fondly to these days when thinking was not forbidden in New York City, and civilized discourse was not yet a vanishing art.

I didn't always stay home at night. This was, after all, the era of Mayor Jimmy Walker, a slim, dapper Irishman who scornfully referred to a reformer as "a guy who rides through a sewer in a glass-bottom boat." Like many a New Yorker, he frequented the mob-run speakeasies which flourished during the days of Prohibition. If you could slip out of your house, it was not really a trick, however young you were, to get by the barred door of a club. A knock at the door brought the eye of a bouncer to the peephole; a cursory inspection of the proffered membership card permitted entry to a world filled with the swirl of smoke, the blast of music, and the rattle of ice in glasses filled with liquor of dubious origin. In other words, it was paradise. At dens of iniquity like the Onyx or the Club Napoleon, one might see Jack "Legs" Diamond, a notorious murderer, or Owney Madden, a rum-runner and gangster whose hand I once shook. The unquestioned queen of nightclubs was Texas

Guinan, née Mary Louise Cecilia Guinan. Her club, El Fay, was bankrolled by racketeer Larry Fay: she would stand at the door and greet patrons with a welcoming smile, shouting, "Hello, suckers!" A native of Waco, Texas, she always insisted, with some logic, that her clubs did not have to sell liquor to make money. She claimed that her customers had flasks and her profits came from cover charges, mineral water, and ginger ale. Those were the days when a nightclub could charge for a bottle of White Rock club soda what a quart of Scotch or bourbon had cost before Prohibition.

Even so, the federal district attorney, Emory R. Bruckner, christening himself "The Avenging Angel," fervently trumpeted that he would bury any nightclub that sold liquor. He immediately dispatched his armaments to the "300" Club, where Texas was the hostess. As they led her away to the paddy wagon, she asked the club's orchestra to play "The Prisoner's Song." Within a month, she was cleared in federal court and opened a successful revue, *The Padlocks of 1927*, to mock her brief incarceration. Such was her reputation that in 1945 she was portrayed by Betty Hutton in the film *Incendiary Blonde*.

My friend Fred Schwed claimed that he was born at a large Eastern prep school when he was 17. I now know what he meant. It is not that kids don't have experiences or ideas; they have the same experiences and the wrong ideas. Let me pass over the rest of my adolescence in silence: I went to high school, fell in love, did all the things one is supposed to do; and then, one day, found myself magically on the campus of College of the City of New York at the age where I was prepared to be taken seriously.

This was not some beautiful Princeton campus with the frosh wearing little beanies, with its distractions of the luncheon and drinking clubs that were part of the privileged college landscape. This was a student body which, for the most part, was trying to climb out of the ghetto. Students commuted from the five boroughs of New York City to take advantage of the opportunities offered by this great educational institution. The sole purpose in coming to City College was to learn.

The hallways and classrooms were not filled with good-looking, two-hundred-and-ten-pound kids who proposed to go on to fame and fortune as figures in basketball or football. Our best basketball players weighed in at one-hundred-and-forty-five pounds. The rivalry between City College and St. John's produced some of the most exciting basketball played at that time. Nat Holman, coach of City College in the 1930s, had been one of the great professional players. For the most part, however, all the students' time was taken up in classrooms that brooked no nonsense and provided enormous learning opportunities.

More intent on debate than on eating from the brown paper bags brought from home, students convened for lunch in a series of alcoves which grouped together those of like political persuasion. Less than a decade after the Russian Revolution, politics was a serious business. Bolshevism was touted as the wave of the future in stimulating and intense dialogue. Although there were vast differences among the groups, by the standards of the 1920s we were all left of center. I lunched in Alcove Two, with one ear trained on the moralizing of the Trotskyites in Alcove One and the rantings of the Stalinists in Alcove Three. The denizens of Alcove Two were unpopular with the others because we coolly and analytically challenged their beliefs. One immediately noticed that the weaker the factual foundation, the more emphasis was placed on loudly quoting flimsy sources. Volume, it seemed, would invest data with the aura of authenticity. The less you knew about something, the more forceful should be your delivery. Alcove Two remained skeptical.

The curriculum itself failed to spark any fires in me until I sat in on Morris Raphael Cohen's philosophy class. It was simply impossible to start a discussion on any topic that did not cause him to zero in with the *brio* of a linebacker chasing a quarterback. He would typically dash in with a disquisition that displayed breathtakingly detailed knowledge. There seemed to be no end to the treasury of his wisdom or his ability to articulate it.

I spearheaded a campaign to puncture, or at least temporarily deflate, Professor Cohen's infuriating omniscience. I was determined to find some obscure minutiae with which to ensnare the erudite pedagogue. After diligent research, my classmates and I located an obscure passage in the *Encyclopedia Britannica* concerning some peculiarities of the religious rites of Africa's Masai tribe. Now our detailed knowledge would rule supreme and surely bring about our academician's defeat.

In class the next day, I seized a moment during a discussion of the dancing dervishes of Islam, and innocently queried as to whether or not this was in some sense the kind of belief in witchcraft that was prevalent in Africa. The air was instantly filled with a spirited intellectual exchange involving the entire class. Such a thing had never before occurred. Wisdom soared around the room, bouncing from wall to floor to ceiling. Professor Cohen stood with mouth agape, dumbstruck. Twenty minutes later, having enjoyed our performance to the fullest, and wanting to savor the reaction, I remarked to Professor Cohen that he had been surprisingly quiet. Without meaning to be impolite, I observed that he had not added much, if anything, to the discussion.

He stood in silence for a moment and then said, "I am profoundly impressed with your erudition. I am humbled by the privilege of teaching so learned a group of students. Moreover, I am flattered to see that you gentlemen have read my wee writing in the *Encyclopedia Britannica*." After class, on the remote possibility that he was putting us on, we dashed for the library and the encyclopedia. Sure enough, the article bore the initials MRC.

Sometime in the late 1970s, I learned that a very intelligent and charming woman seated next to me at dinner was the niece of Morris Raphael Cohen. I began to animatedly recount the Masai saga. Her upraised hand cut me off, as she informed me, "My uncle lived well into his nineties. As he was getting older, I visited him each Sunday, and each Sunday, with a twinkle in his eye, he would ask me: 'Did I ever tell you what happened with those kids at City College?' I would listen patiently, as if it were the first time, and laugh in the appropriate places. As you can see, I don't really need to hear it again. I am, however, glad to meet the smart aleck."

In all honesty, I can lay no claims to having been a star student. That role was reserved for my younger brother Albert, recognized by all around him as a prodigious talent well before he went on to become a renowned mathematical logician and defense intellectual. At seventeen, while a student at City College, he wrote an article for an egghead magazine called *Philosophy of Science*. The piece, entitled "The Structure of the Proposition and the Fact," immediately attracted interest from intelligentsia in all parts of the globe.

One of the epistles which found its way to our door was from a professor at Princeton University, a certain Albert Einstein. The world-famous scientist considered the article to be the most lucid extrapolation of mathematical logic he had ever read. He invited my brother to Princeton to take tea and discuss the paper. When my brother arrived at the great man's home, Frau Einstein arrived at the door, knitting in hand, and (no doubt expecting an elderly academic) asked after my brother's business. "I am Albert Wohlstetter. I have an appointment with the professor." The good lady called out over the sound of her husband's violin playing, "Albert! Another Albert to see you!"

2

NINETEEN TWENTY-NINE

The winter of 1929 was prophetically bleak. Although the crash in the stock market was still six months in the future, the underlying economy gave little cause for cheer. And now that hanging around City College had failed to produce a potential Nobel Laureate in me, I was faced with our family version of affirmative action, a social manifesto that was articulated in a simple declarative statement by my older brother: "Get a job if you want to eat." The objective was not all that easy to achieve, but after numerous setbacks, I was finally hired in February as a runner in the Wall Street firm of Charles R. Hammerslough & Co., salary: $13 a week. (A runner is just a fancy name for an errand boy who delivers securities and other colorful papers to brokers and banks around town.)

Charles Hammerslough had spent his early working years with Augustus Pitou, a theatrical producer of some minor distinction. Charles married into a very wealthy family who thought it inappropriate for their son-in-law to be engaged in so vulgar an activity as show business, so they set him up in Wall Street, to which all families exiled sons who were not qualified to become legitimate businessmen. (It is perhaps worth noting that the office boy in Pitou's office was Moss Hart.)

My first few months in the financial community were almost a blur. The stock market, which I am quite sure nobody, including the head of our firm, clearly understood, roared ahead as if powered by rockets. Brokerage firms were enriched and expanded without ever considering the undeniable fact that new certificates were printed every day. Timber was plentiful and there was no shortage of paper in sight. Everything seemed to confirm Robert Sarnoff's elegant aphorism, "Finance is the fine art of passing currency from hand to hand until it has disappeared."

Credit was freely available. The more actively one traded, the less of one's own capital was required. Brokers vied for the commissions. Big players frequently were on eighty to ninety percent margin. To my skeptical eye, this looked like a pretty dumb idea. Afflicted by a weakness for contrary opinion that occasionally led me into tall grass, I was uncertain of my ability to survive in this wonderland. As it was, I received on-the-job training, which in turn developed my ability to discern on any particular day whether or not a deal was going down the drain.

The nabobs of Wall Street, a generation earlier than mine, had been Thomas Fortune Ryan, John Keene, Barney Baruch, and James Duke. These were the men who created the Tobacco Trust and the Sugar Trust and fought the battle with E. H. Harriman for control of the Union Pacific Railroad. Harriman was a very sharp pirate. When the Vanderbilts, in the person of Jay Gould, sold the Erie Railroad to the New York Central, they were caught in a short position and had bought more stock than had been issued. They were cornered, so Gould simply went out and printed more of those handsome certificates! Ultimately, these were outlawed by the SEC, but not before the Vanderbilts had to make a substantial settlement to Harriman.

When I arrived on the scene, there was a new breed in control: Jesse Livermore, Joseph P. Kennedy, W.C. Durand, Arthur Cutten, Ben Smith, and Louis Kaiser. Kaiser was a notorious market manipulator. He had friends in banks that held securities for their investors but did not trade them. If, for example, a customer had two hundred thousand shares of Consolidated Edison, Kaiser would use his influence to determine that these shares were pledged against a loan for, say, four million dollars. Having identified the existence of a loan that was rather thin at the bank, he would start a bear raid on the stock until the bank was forced to inform the borrower they were going to sell him out if he didn't have any more margin. Kaiser would just stand there with his basket while the stock poured into it. It was a brilliant, if somewhat crooked way of making a living, but Wall Street in the late twenties was a frontier populated with cowboys.

Many of these financiers were throwbacks to the phenomenon of the robber barons, engaged in an entirely different business: the operation of pools. This was the ignoble enterprise of fleecing unsuspecting yokels, not excluding friends. The most despised person in that lot was probably Joseph P. Kennedy, who was perceived by most, even in a den of thieves, as too shady to join with in a common venture.

Pools were consortiums which people organized, sometimes with shares in non-existent companies. They would then begin extolling the great future of, let us say, Coney Island Sand or Trans Continental Toll Bridges. Word would be passed through press agents or media people, whom they bribed, that this stock was a real winner.

Their wives would give dinner parties to prepare their

guests for a fleecing. One of the females would corner the pool operator and ask him for a hot tip whose profits might take the shape of a mink stole. He might suggest Coney Island Sand. "Why don't you buy two hundred shares and I will guarantee you against loss, but I am depending upon you not to tell your husband or your friends."

The woman would then, of course, immediately confide her inside information to her husband, who would buy five thousand shares of the stock. Favored friends would, in turn, ensnare their husbands. When the stock ultimately became worthless, the hosts of this genteel pastime would feign outrage and threaten to bring the majesty of the law on the heads of the villainous management. In the meantime, like the gentlemen they were, they would reimburse the unknowing shill for the loss on her two hundred shares of stock. It doesn't take a mathematical logician to see it was not an impossible way to get rich. The scam followed an age-old formula: set the mark, make the sting, get out of town. And since there was no S.E.C. then, it was possible for people to get together and form these non-existent corporations, to buy a company that used to be in the shovel business, for instance, and give it a fancy name. Nobody looked at the balance sheets. You didn't even have to have an accountant, because nobody asked. Everyone was caught up in a new national pastime: play the market, get something for nothing. Almost no-one succeeded but, like playing the horses, the compulsion to gamble was overpowering. (They even got a very attractive certificate to frame and hang on the wall!) That was ere we all learned that Armageddon makes regular appearances at the Stock Exchange.

There is the tale of a country cousin from Iowa visiting his relatives in New York. On a tour of the financial district, the New Yorker proudly pointed to the great buildings that made Wall Street a canyon and said, "You see those buildings? That's where the brokers' offices are." Then, turning his cousin's attention to J. P. Morgan & Co., at 23 Wall Street, where a line of Rolls-Royces awaited their owners at the close of market, he said, "You see those Rolls-Royces? They belong to the brokers." They ambled to the foot of Manhattan, near Battery Park, and looked out over the water's edge. The New Yorker pointed to the yachts riding at anchor, including the *Corsair*, owned by J. P. Morgan. "Those are the brokers' yachts." The boy from Iowa hesitated a moment, then asked politely, "Where are the customers' yachts?" Later, my friend Fred Schwed wrote a howlingly funny book entitled *Where Are the Customers' Yachts?*

Fred was a rather dumpy little man, but he had the most ribald and quick-witted sense of humor. He was one of the few people I knew who was genuinely suspicious of the market activity in the fateful summer of 1929, although he was renowned for being a gambler. Every day, rain or shine, he walked from the New York Curb Exchange to meet a member of the New York Stock Exchange. There, the rivals would solemnly flip a hundred dollar gold piece in a best-of-five bet. Fred's other claim to fame was that he had been kicked out of Princeton three weeks before graduation for having a girl in his room; these days, of course, they kick you out if you *don't* have a girl in your room.

Within a matter of weeks, I had risen to the back office as a clerk, although I had the helpless premonition that I was sitting in a temporary shelter that would soon disintegrate. I therefore kept my eye on the want-ad section of the *Times*, where I actually saw an advertisement by my own employer, petitioning for a junior trader. I had noted that traders seemed to be a highly respected category of people and were accordingly paid more than my $13 a week stipend.

So it was that, on Monday morning, bright and early, I took the vacant seat in the trading room. I announced for all to hear that I was the new junior trader. Hammerslough looked at me a moment and made me a sporting proposition: "Keep the seat and follow carefully the instructions given to you, which, with any luck, will be in understandable form. If you are error-free for the day, you will become a junior trader at a salary of $30 a week. On the other hand, if you foul it up just once, you are not a trader, a clerk or a runner; you are a short-lived memory to the firm, and you'd better look for another job." Even the most ordinary minds held the naïve but indestructible belief that they could forecast the future, and, after all, my mind was as ordinary as the next.

I found no difficulty in deciphering the tape, which in those days was paper. After listening to our own traders, I decided that, if possible, they knew less than I did, although they were more familiar with the lingo. It should be remembered that in those days, the trading rooms were not filled with the Harvard business school types one finds today. The majority of traders were not college graduates; it was really after the Second World War that college enrollment zoomed up enormously. Wall Street was a mecca for people with a gambler's instinct and an auctioneer's attitude. Since reading was an almost unknown activity for most of them, anyone who could read without moving his lips qualified as an intellectual. Among these types I soon became the source of considerable wisdom in a space inhabited by fifteen or sixteen contemporaries. Bogged down by the delusion that only dullards studied, they tried to survive by their wits. Since they were missing the essential ingredient, most proved to be unequal to the task.

Almost no one paid attention to the newspapers, which, with stories of bankruptcies and job layoffs, semaphored an impending collision with reality. Brokers were too busy counting paper profits to evaluate the impact of the daily news on the industry, or the economy in general. Instead of alarm bells, only self-congratulatory chimes went off in the heads of the optimists. By June 1929, I had become the manager of the trading department.

The market continued to surge, although the public had not gotten the message about more than a few shell companies. Our firm dealt mainly in bank and insurance stocks, which were regarded with religious fervor as safe investments. The phenomenon of other stocks headed for the tank escaped the notice of our savants. During July and August, I tried to work up enough nerve to recite the speech that would shatter their dreams, but jobs were hard to get. It was easier to go along.

One fateful day, the ticker printed a transaction of five thousand shares of General Motors at a new high. Charles Hammerslough let out a roar of triumph and proclaimed that everything was going to five thousand! I confronted Mr. Hammerslough and said, "You are the third person I know who said something like that. Some were farmers in the Midwest three years ago. You told me that you turned down a chance to invest in *Abie's Irish Rose*. That made millions and also proved that you too could be wrong. Unless you want to go back into show business, I think we should play the short side of the market."

His normally pale complexion flushed a rosy red, and he unleashed his wrath with all the delicacy born of good breeding and the Ivy League schools, screaming, "You little son of a bitch! You have been in the business for a grand total of four-and-a-half months, and apparently you have been endowed with some heretofore unknown superior source of information. My first inclination is to kick your ass out of here, but instead I am removing you as the head of our trading department. And second, I am going to give you fifty thousand dollars and the room at the far end of the corridor. There, you can play the short side to your heart's content, and when you have lost all your money, come back and see me. I will then determine whether or not we have a job for you."

This was a critical point in my life. I watched Charlie Hammerslough join the fanatical crowd of optimists, ignroring all signs of approaching doom. Of course, Charlie should have known better; he was a carnie, a show biz type and here he was being taken in by his own hype. He was carried away by the jumping tape; when he looked up, he never saw that this, like every other market, had a ceiling. Well, I knew life wasn't like that. In my own father's case, I had seen the plug pulled from a sure-fire money-making machine.

On Tuesday, October 29, 1929, everything hit the fan. With a drastic drop in iron and steel production coupled with a sudden rise in British interest rates, all European capital was pulled out of the U.S. market. As is usual in these cases, the damage was (in accordance with Feinberg's Law) unevenly distributed. In the months that followed, everything, good and bad, was in free fall, confirming the age-old adage that when they raid the whorehouse they take all the girls. There were an unprecedented sixteen million shares traded on that day as the Dow Jones Average plummeted more than thirty points. Speculators were forced to sell everything they had bought on margin and $30 billion disappeared overnight, a sum equal to the entire dollar cost of America's involvement in the First World War.

When the market opened with an almost audible rush that morning, Charles Hammerslough immediately called me up to the trading room. There was absolute pandemonium. Every telephone was ringing. People were racing around, trying frantically to stem the tide; no one could believe what was happening. I was in the middle of a transaction with a man called Paul Bower when I looked up and, to my horror, saw a man's body plummet past the window. It was an elderly gentleman from the customer's room, a pleasant-looking fellow I had often seen going in and out of 120 Broadway: people had told me that he was a great trader. Afterwards, of course, everyone made jokes: "Don't walk too close to the buildings, because . . . ," but many people were unable to face the realities of the Crash and stepped out for that short walk on the window ledge. Up until then, I thought of what I was doing as a kind of game; now came the rude awakening: what we did had an effect, a real impact on many lives.

The bankers at J. P. Morgan intervened in an effort to stabilize the free fall of the market. By personally appearing on the floor of the Exchange and buying stocks in major corporations, they exerted a calming effect. As the market began to crawl up again I continued to trade small and took little advantage of the upswing. But I did not take some of the hits that others did. The Crash had a sobering effect on many who thought themselves cognizant of the market. They may have been privy to inside knowledge, but even that advantage was not enough to save them. Information was suddenly unreliable until proven otherwise. For me, the Crash was a defining moment of my life. Skepticism was no longer merely a matter of personal disposition, or even philosophy; it was a necessary instrument of survival.

As over-the-counter firms went, Hammerslough's had been quite well capitalized, yet by December 31, 1929, the only capital remaining in the firm was in my account. I had not made a great fortune, since many of the sales I made fell victim to the bankruptcy of the purchasers. At the end, however, I had my $50,000 and a small amount in excess. I had no particular mentor at Hammerslough's, but Charles himself would give me a handful of stocks and compare the results I had to that of other brokers in the house. Gradually, I was granted more authority and I began to set the tone for the other brokers. It was a learning process, but a broker isn't made overnight.

Some people I knew did not fare as well as I. My good friend, Fred Schwed, was in Europe when the Crash hit. His brokers, Oppenheimer and Company, had cabled him in September that unless he put up more margin they would sell his account, which they did. This took virtually all of Fred's fortune, but, gambler that he was, he had an ace up his sleeve. He had given $2 million in Treasury Bonds to his lovely wife Birdie, with the strict instructions that this was to be used only in the direst emergency. No greater emergency was possible than the Crash, so Fred cashed in his bonds and invested in a real estate venture on Rockaway Island. I suppose it's almost redundant to say that the venture failed and Fred went bankrupt.

A painfully sad result of the Crash was its effect on Fred Schwed's father. This venerable man had owned beautiful property on Long Island with horses running in his backyard; now he was penniless. In desperation, he came to me for help, and with tears in his eyes said, "I've outlived my usefulness. Take some advice: don't make my mistakes." It was so painful to see this noble and charming gentleman brought so low. At the time he came to me I had my own firm with two associates, so I gave him a job for two years at the ludicrous rate of thirty-five dollars per week. I could hardly afford to pay him, and it was certainly humiliating for him to take such a menial amount, but I could not turn my back on a man who had accepted me at his board as if I were his son. He had value to me as a business associate because of his contacts on the Street; but, more importantly, he had value to me as a man.

✧ ✧ ✧

During the Crash, the financial giants of yore awakened each morning in a fine sweat and with their bed sheets tangled around them. Those who hung on were convinced that, like the slaughter of the first-born in Egypt, this was punishment for past offenses. They clung to the notion that, as the Red Sea had opened and closed, the market would rebound and there would be a happy ending after all. There were continuing optimistic prognoses from all manner of apparently reliable sources. "Hysteria has now disappeared from Wall Street," announced the *Times* of London (Nov. 21, 1929). "1930 will be a splendid employment year," predicted the Department of Labor. "I see nothing in the present situation that is either menacing or warrants pessimism," intoned the Secretary of the Treasury, Andrew Mellon, "I have every confidence there will be a revival of activity in the Spring." J. P. Morgan himself remarked rather archly, "I don't know anything about a depression." Unfortunately, not even scopolamine could have elicited the truth, for no one contemplated anything so unimaginable. The real condition of the economy was quite unknown to everyone except gypsy palm readers and interpreters of the zodiac signs.

Charles R. Hammerslough & Co. limped along until the second, more devastating crash in April of 1930. Fortunately, I had remained skeptical of the marketplace, and our modest capital remained intact. What did disappear, however, was every employee of the firm except for Mr. Hammerslough and myself. We moved into the offices of a Stock Exchange firm, Frank B. Cahn & Co., which monitored our books and cleared our transactions for a fee. There was a great deal of office space available for sublet. Charlie and I shared a single desk at Frank Cahn's small office during the first few years after the Crash. We installed private wires to other trading houses in the Street, and I managed to eke out a rather precarious living. Charlie suffered no undue hardship as his wife's family, the Rittenbergers, retained a reasonable portion of the wealth from their great textile business.

This rather unpromising environment persisted for about two years, until Charlie Hammerslough announced that he was surrendering. He sued for peace by renouncing Wall Street forever. When Charles said he was leaving, I felt some degree of relief. I was essentially supporting him, as was the capital his father-in-law had given him. We made a modest living, but Charlie was not a creative thinker or a very good trader. I felt that I owed it to him to stick with him for all that he had done for me in the past, but after he quit, I felt that I was a free man.

At this time, Theodore Prince & Co. was a major force in trading in Wall Street. Their retail office called me one morning and requested a quote on Chase Bank (bank stocks had reached low levels never dreamed possible; National City Bank, the forerunner of Citicorp, had plummeted from about $450 in October 1929 to a price close to $10 in the latter part of 1932). I quoted the bid and ask as $12 to $12¼. At that moment, my other phone rang. It was Prince & Co.'s trading department, also asking for a quote on Chase, which I repeated. My left ear, connected with the sales department, heard, "I will sell you five hundred shares at $12," and simultaneously, my right ear picked up the information that their trading department would buy five hundred shares at $12¼. I confirmed each transaction, and carefully time-stamped the transaction sheet.

Later that same afternoon, I presented myself at Mr. Prince's office where I laid on his desk the report on those two transactions, and pointed out the identical time stamps. Mr. Prince, who was a very distinguished-looking gent wearing pince-nez glasses, asked me to explain this remarkable event, and, as modestly as I could, I suggested that he needed some-body who could re-organize his trading department.

Mr. Prince said, "Well, young man, I assume you are not here as a good citizen, but would like the job?" I admitted that he had discovered the purpose of my visit, and in a falsely con-fident voice, I requested a salary of one hundred fifty dollars a week, which was a tidy sum in 1930, plus five percent of the profit of the new department. After a look of astonishment, he instructed me to return the next day at 9:00 A.M., enter his pri-vate office, and write on a piece of paper the lowest figure I would accept. He admonished that I wasn't to disappoint him by quoting the silly amount I had just recited. These, after all, were difficult times.

The next morning, right on schedule, I left a note with the exact same terms on Mr. Prince's desk, also pointing out that my first model transaction, which might be duplicated several times a day, would have cost him one hundred and twenty-five dollars. The following Monday, I became the manager of the bank and insurance stock-trading department of Theodore Prince & Co., at a weekly salary of one hundred fifty dollars.

I was now situated in the innermost trading room with more than fifty people trading stocks and bonds. I sat at a master tur-ret that connected phones with every brokerage house whose wires terminated at our firm. A directive was issued that any re-quest from another firm dealing in bank or insurance stocks must be instantly transferred to my turret command.

The years 1930 through 1932 saw volume on the New York Stock Exchange at a level of six hundred thousand to nine hun-dred thousand shares per day. Compared to today's two hun-dred million shares per day, it is obvious that every trade we made was a partial determinant of the quality of our home menu for the week. Long-range prognoses became unnecessary baggage. If the shares did not perform in accordance with one's original judgment, a speedy exit was essential for survival, as divine intervention was unlikely. A useful bit of wisdom I absorbed is known as "The Rule of the Hole." When you are in a hole, stop digging. It may also be expressed as "The first loss is the best loss." I also remember at this time asking Benjamin Graham, "If you are long on a stock and take a licking on it, should you sell it even if you still believe in it?" Ben (founder of the Graham-Newman investment fund corporation and author of a pioneering book on security analysis) replied, "Don't get trapped into thinking there is a finite measure of what a stock is worth. Stocks are only worth what you can sell them for; they are not worth a multiple of anything." I always found this analysis based on a stock's book value to be sage advice.

Prior to my arrival at Theodore Prince & Co., the bank and insurance stocks were handled by a single employee, a man of forty or thereabouts who appeared to have little interest or ambition in doing anything more exciting or potentially more lucrative. Shortly after he became my assistant I found out why. At one time or another, we might buy for our own account one thousand shares of Bankers Trust, not looking for long-term gains. A day or so later, the stock might have moved up $1\frac{1}{2}$ points, at which time I would tell my assistant to sell seven hundred shares of Bankers Trust and keep three hundred. He would inform me that he had sold the stock earlier that day at a point below its present market. This was certainly possible, although it began to happen too often. I watched things very closely, and finally realized that this brazen assistant of mine ran his own private business right under my nose. When the market was at a low point, he would time-stamp a blank sale slip and, in pencil, note the price of the stock at that time. If the afternoon brought an improving market and a rise of one dollar in the stock, he would fill in the sale slip prepared that morning. I verified this by watching his performance for a couple of days.

Before I had a chance to tackle and disembowel his personal enterprise, he said, "Look, before we talk, would you just come with me for a few minutes?" We arrived at the office of a scarcely-known trading house where I was introduced to the senior partner. He slipped an envelope into my hand, in which I found $1,500 in brand-new bills. He then gave me a friendly pat on the back and said, "There's plenty more where that came from." I returned the envelope, restraining myself from stuffing it down his throat. I rebuked my assistant and told him to take a walk to the nearest exit, and I advised his confederate that if I ever saw his name on Theodore Prince's books, I would have him placed in durance vile. This behavior went unprosecuted but the culprit left the business and went to live in Florida on his ill-gotten gains. I didn't think of myself as being particularly righteous; I just wanted to put a stop to anything which might have damaged me or the firm very severely.

Life on the Street occasionally raised some smiles, too. Arthur D. Lipper and Company was a great firm named for a tubby old man with large Germanic mustaches and his irrevocably dumb son. The senior Lipper and I were in the steam room of the City Athletic Club one day with some of his cronies, towels wrapped around our heads. Earlier that day, someone had placed an order with Lippers to buy a contract for thirty bushels of wheat, and Arthur Junior thought that "thirty wheat" meant thirty contracts. Wheat went through the stratosphere as there was nationwide panic buying and selling, especially in the wheat pits in Chicago. The mistake was finally cleared up later in the day, but at considerable cost to Lipper and Company. Through the steam of the club sauna somebody asked old man Lipper, "Arthur, what's the dope on the floor?" Arthur shot back, "My son!"

Most of the guys who wore carnations in their buttonholes, bought the first roadsters, and flashed their money clips had been trading on very thin margins and the Crash swept them away. But there was always a new stream of brassy and breezy hustlers rushing forth to take their places. I remember once walking past a trader's desk and overhearing a conversation between a broker and the poor slob in Ireland to whom he was trying to sell a bond: "Now, Mr. O'Malley, what I am offering you is a bond that will be paid off in forty years in gold. This is not a secured note, this is . . . " (dramatic pause) " . . . a debenture!" A debenture is merely a promissory note; there is nothing behind it. And yet the way that this exotic word rolled off the broker's tongue was enough to evoke for any hapless sucker the fabled cities of El Dorado or the lost treasure of the Incas.

A couple of my friends, Joe Klingenstein and Bernie Rubinger, who were connected through family with two of the great investment houses, suggested that the three of us form a partnership. I had only accumulated a modest amount of capital myself, but, in those days, that was sufficient. The senior partner of one of the firms was uncle to one of my new partners, and he assured me that my fortunes would improve if I solved the family problem of what to do with a troublesome nephew. At the end of 1932, we formed our over-the-counter brokerage firm, with capital around $4,000, but with assurances that much more was available. My name was now on the door of a new brokerage house: Rubinger Wohlstetter & Co.

Our timing was designed for a fiasco. We threw our portals open exactly one week before March 4, 1933, the day of President Roosevelt's inauguration. One week later, the President closed the banks. Here I was, the senior partner of a Wall Street firm, leaving my home in the morning not in a Rolls-Royce but on the IRT subway, clutching a brown paper bag containing two sandwiches and a piece of cake. I also had fifteen cents from my mother that would pay the five cents in each direction subway fare and an additional five cents to buy an apple. This fruit was very easy to obtain, since every street corner had some forlorn former vice-president selling some.

The morning headlines trumpeted what we all knew: FDR INAUGURATED. Seated in the subway, I read the papers and wondered how many American voters really understood the consequences of what the new government had promised, regardless of what Roosevelt might actually deliver. I had long ago concluded that the intellectual level of the electorate was the equivalent of a Tootsie Roll's™. FDR was certain to appeal to the public's candy store mentality. I was confident, however, that our new Mahatma would overturn the thirteen-year old Volstead Act. That would be the perfect bon-bon for the voters: Repeal Prohibition!

But how to capitalize on this notion? I was not in the booze business, and my closest contact had been some surreptitious visits to speakeasies, where a brown bituminous liquid passed for anything from Scotch to bourbon.

120 Broadway, which housed our offices, had a much larger and more distinguished tenant, Abraham & Co., now part of Lehman Bros., an international brokerage house well connected in London as well as in New York. In their library, I searched out statistics on English distilling companies. Information was scant, and White Horse Scotch was the only name I recognized. The name of the parent company was Distillers Corporation Ltd., so I made inquiries as to the market in the stock in London.

Much to my surprise, I discovered that the London Stock Exchange was not a continuous market, meaning that they could not trade with the alacrity of the NYSE. Although there were so-called jobbers, orders to buy or sell would create the necessity for brokers to seek out the other side of any transaction. This process could take a couple of days in an inactive stock. It also disclosed eyebrow-raising possibilities, particularly the rather interesting ability to buy an option on a block of shares for as short a time frame as twenty-four hours. The cost of an option for so limited a period in an inactive stock was minuscule. I bought an option on ten thousand shares, starting at the next day's opening of the marketplace in New York, for the huge sum of $500.

Arriving at my office, I commissioned the printing of the sketchy information I had collected on penny postcards. I then took a tombstone ad in the financial pages of *The New York Times* and *The Wall Street Journal*. The message was short and to the point:

DISTILLERS CORPORATION LTD.
BOUGHT, SOLD AND QUOTED

Our firm name modestly appeared beneath.

The following morning, before the market opened, I received a call from Charles Mitchell, chairman of the National City Bank, asking what Distillers Corporation Ltd. was all about. With all the assurance born of ignorance, I told him of the ambrosias which would soon be available to all drunks and novitiates prepared to study the art of drinking hard liquor.

Mitchell asked whether I had anything in writing about the company, and I agreed to deliver my precious little information to him. He then requested the bid and ask price of the stock. My option translated into about $14\frac{1}{4}$ per share in American money. I did, however, have a very interesting thing going for me: since there had been no American depository receipts issued, no one in the United States could sell me the stock. Taking a deep breath, I said the market was $15\frac{3}{4}$ bid, offered at $16\frac{1}{4}$. Mitchell thought that he should buy one thousand shares. I obliged him by selling it to him at $16\frac{1}{4}$.

I was now in the rather favorable position of being short one thousand shares of stock at $16\frac{1}{4}$ with an option to buy that stock at $14\frac{1}{4}$, and I now had a safe bid. The next call was from the senior partner of another banking house who obliged by buying another thousand shares.

I can only describe that day as the triumph of hope over sanity. Before the day ended, I had bought an option on another ten thousand shares and awaited the next morning, feeling for all the world as if my fortune were already made.

The next day started well enough, and we were very soon almost complete with our sales, but the nature of our callers had significantly changed. Our phone lines were clogged with calls from European and American arbitrageurs. It was clear that the jig was up. Taking our cue from Longfellow's "The Day Is Done," we determined to fold our tents like the Arabs and, as silently, steal away.

This should have been the end of a rather successful adventure, but the fate that takes care of fools and audacious men intervened to grant us an additional bonus. Apparently, Joe Klingenstein of Wertheim and Company had been thinking for some time about the Distillers Company, but I had, by virtue of my swift action, pre-empted his strike on the market. When he realized that someone within his own ranks was selling the stock from under his nose he abruptly summoned me to his office.

Klingenstein was the very same Uncle Joe of the partner who had created our association and he now asked me how much we had profited in the preceding day and a half. I shyly confirmed that we had already made about $43,000 on a $4,000 capital investment. His eyes popped open, and he looked at me as if seeing me for the first time. "All right," he said. "What do you want?" I told him that all I really wanted from him was the opportunity to perform his market transactions for a brokerage commission. He agreed, but then said, "I want you to take that money you made today and buy a seat on the New York Curb Exchange" (now known as the American Stock Exchange). "Do it before you lose it," was the admonition. He suggested that we put his nephew on the floor, but that I should stay in the office where he could not only be in immediate contact with me, but also keep an eye on me. I let that pass. Our new venture had taken on the dignity of membership in the New York Curb Exchange.

1933 turned into a boon year for the liquor industry. After the repeal of Volstead and the ratification of the Twenty-first Amendment there was a veritable explosion of new breweries and distilleries. Within a year, National Distillers, Schenley Distillers, Frankfort Distilleries (later bought out by Seagrams), and Hiram Walker, Inc. had begun to pour over twenty different brands of whiskey down thirsty American gullets. During Prohibition, it was estimated that illegal sales had topped one and a half billion gallons of hard liquor. Imagine what legalization did! In addition to liquor, of course, beer sales went through the roof.

Soft drinks, however, took a terrible tumble.

Micro- and macroeconomics were as much an enigma in 1929 as they are today. With all the great computers now available, one man's guess is still as good as another's. President Hoover and his cabinet kept assuring us that prosperity was just around the corner (although they did not specify which corner). In retrospect, of course, Hoover was proved right, though he was eleven years early.

3

ON THE TOWN

During the mid-thirties, expansion on the New York Curb Exchange, my company was so busy executing orders in common shares that we needed the part-time services of somebody to philander in the bond department. We fixed upon an ordinary young man who nonetheless sported a certain cachet. Harold Kriendler, affectionately called Pete, was the brother of no less an eminento than Jack Kriendler, who along with Charlie Berns owned one of the most famous boîtes in the world. It is still known as Jack and Charlie's, the club's name before it moved uptown to 21 West 52nd Street.

No business contacts that anyone could have brought to the firm would have been as welcome to me as the favorable notice that Pete now obtained for me with Luigi, the *maitre d'hotel* at his brother's den; for at "21" there was a caste system that rivaled that of India. Habitués were seated in accordance with a

secret formula the nature of which was known only to the proprietors and Luigi. The uninitiated lived in perpetual bewilderment, trying to unravel the rules that permitted a person to
move up the scale to the elite part of the room. Big tips to the
maître d' would not help (fortunately for me since my income
was fluctuating; my entertainment budget was perpetually in
the red; my white tie and tails rented; and my ambition for the
evening was to retain enough money to take the subway back
home). No, mere money was not the answer. The secret was
written in Sanskrit.

Upon entering 21 West 52nd Street, guests were met by
two well-dressed but rather formidable gentlemen, who greeted
the familiar faces and treated them in a very deferential manner.
If you wandered in off the street, thinking this was just another
saloon, you would be politely informed that all tables were
booked, and encouraged to visit Toots Shor's on the next block.
There, they catered to the sporting trade, the racing set, and
some of the vaudeville comedians, and the competition between
the two clubs was intense.

The bar on the main floor at "21" was fashioned after a
grand old English pub. Beer steins and miniature models of favored clients' products hung from the ceiling: model airplanes,
locomotives, oil trucks, tractors, and telephones. The walls
were decorated with original drawings by such great magazine
illustrators as Bradford Crandall, Arthur William Brown, and
Peter Arno. Its very comfortable and understated ambiance was
divided in accordance with the three-part system devised by
Jack Kriendler, The Baron.

In the first section, at the left as you came in, were the
power brokers, the social set, big honchos of U.S. Steel or Standard Oil, or the great stars such as Cary Grant and writers like
Herman Mankiewicz. There were also Hollywood moguls and
theater critics such as George Jean Nathan, and writers and

sportscasters like Ted Husing and Robert Benchley. Some tables bore a brass plate on the wall behind, claiming the turf for a special patron. The tables would only be given to someone else if Luigi was certain that its proper owner was elsewhere. A few, such as myself, were exceptions.

Another, more historic, exception involved George Jessel and Lena Horne. Lena was appearing at the Savoy Plaza, a beautiful hotel which occupied the present site of the General Motors building on Fifth Avenue. George, a star vaudevillian, was overwhelmed by Lena's performance, and asked that she join his party at the table, only to receive a short reply stating that it was the management's policy not to permit entertainers to sit at tables with guests.

George was not to be outdone and invited her to dinner at "21" two nights later. At the door of the club, the designated greeter, Monty, was somewhat taken aback and blurted out "Do you have a reservation, Sir?" George said, "Yes, I do." Monty queried, "Who made it?" George dryly replied, "Abraham Lincoln." Fortunately for all, Jack Kriendler came through the dining room at this moment and very warmly greeted George and Lena. It would not have happened at the Stork Club where Josephine Baker was informed that she was unwelcome. In Paris, Miss Baker's ecdysiastic performances blinded French audiences to her color.

The center section of "21" was generally occupied by the young people whose parents occupied the first section, as well as those who did not yet qualify for the front. The final section, far to the right of the entry, was clearly Siberia for those who were acceptable but of no great importance. Optimists who generously crossed Luigi's palm would have been better advised to save their money; the barriers were raised only when Jack or Charlie gave the signal.

In case you are wondering where the hootch was stashed during the Prohibition raids, I can reveal this little secret. In the basement of "21" is a thick wall with no visible door. There is, however, a cunningly concealed keyhole, accessible only to a long, slender key. When the lock clicks, the wall swings open like a bank vault door. And that's where the liquor was stored. It became a practice, in more enlightened times, to lay down a wine in this cellar on the occasion of the birth of your child. When the youngster reached the age of 21, the wine would be opened to celebrate the achievement of majority.

"21" was known as a place that never bought a customer a drink because Charlie Berns, with tongue in cheek, had admonished his bartenders, "Never give away anything you can sell." The fact is, they had very quietly assisted several young men. No one but the Kriendlers and myself knew that I had unwarranted credit when times were difficult.

Once, during a particularly lean period in the mid-thirties, I determined that I could not, for the time being at least, afford the tariff at "21"; reluctantly, I dropped out of sight. About a month later (during which my night life was limited to sharing the RKO movie house with the common folk), Jack called me and asked me why I had not shown up recently. I explained that I couldn't afford the prices at his saloon. Without a moment's hesitation, he uttered words which I will never forget: "You are family, and you come here when you like, with whomever you like, and sign the tab, including the tip. Pay me when you have the money, and if you don't have it, don't worry."

That night, I turned up at "21" with Georgia Caroll, one of the great beauties of the time. We ate a sumptuous repast, had champagne, and were seated at the table near the door, normally accorded to Ted Husing. Georgia was the cynosure of all eyes, which did something for my ego. I had only the twenty-five cents to tip the hatcheck girl, so we walked home, although Georgia had a modeling job early the next morning.

The next morning, feeling it was only fair that I not embarrass such optimists as the Kriendlers and Berns, I called Arnold Daxe, a tailor of my acquaintance, and queried, "What do you do if you have no clothes and no money?" Came the welcome answer, "You come here and order four suits and two overcoats, and pay me if you ever have the money."

In short, I quickly became the best dressed pauper at the classiest joint in New York.

Perhaps the most glamorous place of all was the Central Park Casino where on Sundays, for five dollars, we had tea and brioche and danced to Leo Reisman's orchestra, Eddie Duchin at the piano. Authentic members of society's Four Hundred and descendants of passengers on the Mayflower mingled with the glossy models and stars of stage and screen. Friday and Saturday demanded white tie and tails or tuxedo. The proprietor was Sidney Solomon, a buddy of Mayor James J. Walker, who caused the city to rent the premises to him for a pittance. The lovely Central Park house was founded in the twenties on the southeast corner of 72nd Street and Fifth Avenue. Joseph Urban, one of the great designers of the day, created the most glamorous supper club in the nation. I was a regular Sunday patron.

In 1931, only the very rich could afford the tariff at the Casino. While the cover charge was only two bucks (at a time when the average weekly wage was thirty dollars) a bottle of club soda cost about twenty times the market price. The liquor was provided from a hip flask carried by the celebrant. Compare that price with the fare at Gallagher's, the celebrated steak house, which opened in 1933: a steak dinner *à la carte* cost one dollar and seventy-five cents!

The Casino was a showcase where the grand ladies showed off their Parisian frocks by Mainbocher, Chanel, and all the other great French couturiers. As I looked around the room, I figured that Cartier had delivered their jewels by the barrel.

When Eddie Duchin left the piano between sets, my date and I would walk across the hall with him and play backgammon in the Urban Room until the next set. Eddie was a marvelous musician and altogether a class act. He ultimately replaced Leo Reisman and the orchestra took on his name.

In 1932, Jimmy Walker, having absconded with the maximum amount of graft allowable, left City Hall. According to the investigation by the specially-appointed Seabury Commission, he may have exceeded his level of authority to steal. Amid the usual payoff scandals, Walker fell from grace when it became known that he was living openly with a showgirl at the Mayfair House, even though he was inconveniently entangled in the bonds of matrimony with someone else. For a year, New York had an acting mayor by the name of Joseph V. McKee, although my impression is he never visited City Hall, being quite unable to locate it.

The end of Walker's reign ordained the demise of the plush rendezvous in Central Park. Mr. Solomon left for Mexico for reasons of health and an understandable dislike of answering impertinent questions. Whoever made his thin black ties lost a good customer. Fiorello LaGuardia did not reverse the evaporation of money from the city's coffers, but he proved that he was a superior mayor by reading the funny papers to the kids on the radio whenever the newspapers went on strike.

The Stork Club was founded in 1929 on West 58th Street and Sixth Avenue. Three years later it was moved to 51st Street and Park, before finally nesting, in 1933, in a small house on 53rd Street between Fifth and Madison Avenues. Here it remained until its closure in 1965. After it was demolished, Bill Paley of CBS donated the land to the city for a park in honor of his mother.

The building was not much to look at from the outside, but inside it was attractive, crowded, and noisy. At the height of its celebrity, in the thirties and forties, it was always packed wall to wall, mostly with the younger set dancing to a five-piece band on a floor that was too small for that purpose (though the best entertainment was provided by a popular pianist, Joey Bushkin, who was truly a virtuoso). No one would have described the minuscule up and down movements we were able to make on the crowded dance floor as "tripping the light fantastic." If we had been jammed any closer, it would have qualified as an orgy.

Among the attractions were hundreds of balloons clinging to the ceiling. At about midnight, the balloons would drift downward while the paying customers eagerly reached for them. A large percentage of the balloons contained five, ten, or twenty dollar bills, and there was even one with a hundred dollar bill. Others had certificates entitling the holder to Stork Club perfume, or suspenders with the club logo.

Admission to the Stork Club was by no means automatic; people would be barred for no apparent reason. Many insalubrious characters were admitted, while some of society's finest were left standing in bewilderment on the sidewalk. Reservations were no guarantee either; if the place was packed, an unfamiliar face would be summarily denied access. A swain who failed to finagle his date's admission to the hallowed premises would suffer the anguish of Hamlet, and many a budding romance foundered on the rocks of the Stork's threshold.

The proprietor of all this opulence was an undistinguished boor by the name of Sherman Billingsly, the pride of Oklahoma and a former bootlegger. He was not at all what one would expect in a place that catered to the upper classes, but he did have one thing going for him: the pied piper of the thirties and forties, Walter Winchell, was a regular patron. So assiduously did Billingsly fawn over Winchell that when Walter complained about the volume of the band, Billingsly installed a glass wall near Winchell's table to muffle the noise. There was even a dish, chicken à la Walter Winchell, named for him. Although he wined and dined at his ease, Winchell never picked up a tab.

Winchell was the perfect paradigm of Broadway. Prohibition, nightclubs, machine guns, and revivalists like Billy Sunday and Aimee Semple McPherson were grist for his mill. When he spoke, words tumbled over one another as if he were thinking at the top of his voice, as if he could not contain his inner excitement. He was a truly matchless reporter of human trivia, and inspired a hoard of imitators. As an ex-hoofer, Winchell sensed the wild, brittle tempo of the times, playing Broadway like a fiddle; he made a lot of money doing it, too. Thanks to him, nobody had to look over the transom to see what was going on.

I met Winchell through a young woman called Mary Lou Bentley, a chorus girl who once appeared on stage with my wife Rose (I am jumping ahead into the forties now but I beg the reader's patience and promise to introduce this charming lady in due time). Winchell was still married to his wife June, and was twenty-five years Mary Lou's senior, but there was no denying the attraction of this leggy, blonde knockout from Texas. She had come to New York at the tender age of fifteen to appear in Billy Rose's club, the Casa Mañana, and it was there that Winchell was first smitten by her lissome sexiness. Within a year, the "Long Stemmed Rose," as Mary Lou was known, became Winchell's mistress.

Winchell's column was the bible for café society, show business, and the millions who wanted to feel as if they had inside information. It was gulped down with coffee first thing in the morning, and was so influential that the mere mention of a stock that he liked could make the shares soar two or three points the following day. He could also make and break reputations with a few well-chosen words.

At around midnight, after plugging the Stork Club on his popular radio program, Winchell would hold court at Table 50 in the Cub Room. A mention in Winchell's column made a press agent a hero to his client. But the stringer had to be careful that his allegiance was to Winchell alone. If he ever passed a morsel to Ed Sullivan, for example, he would be banished from Winchell's column forever. Ironically, Sullivan was a columnist for Winchell's old paper, the *Graphic*. Long before his popularity on his Sunday night television show, Sullivan was a well-regarded reporter and radio commentator. Winchell despised him, and Sullivan reciprocated the feeling; their wars in the columns of the press were legendary.

For a very brief time, Sherman Billingsly had his own interview program on radio. Unfortunately, the only book he had read was the Sears catalogue, so the show labored under the influence of comic opera. One of England's great actresses, Estelle Winwood, dined at the Stork Club in 1950 and was persuaded to submit to an interview by Billingsly. Miss Winwood was starring at the Bleecker Street Playhouse in George Bernard Shaw's play, *Mrs. Warren's Profession.* Billingsly read from notes prepared for him and amiably inquired of the incredulous star, "So tell me, what *was* Mrs. Warren's profession?" Understandably, Billingsly's radio career sank beneath the waves with scarcely a ripple.

If I was always ready to defend (somewhat disingenuously to be sure) my penchant for nightlife by citing its benefits to both my business and cultural life, those benefits were nevertheless real enough.

The attention I received at "21" dissipated the pungent fragrance of the subway and paid off in more than trinkets and beads. Many of the nation's great businessmen were assured by Jack and Charlie that I was a very promising young man. I found myself rubbing shoulders with partners in Merrill Lynch and Lehman Kuhn Loeb, and raising a tipple with the chairmen of Chemical and Marine Midland Banks. It was there, too, that I met Robert Benchley and Dorothy Parker, founding members of the infamous Algonquin Round Table; through them, I was introduced to such wondrous wordsmiths as Franklin P. Adams, Carl Sandburg, and Mark Van Doren, to name just a few.

In the mid-thirties, when the Round Tablers were starting to draw apart, Bob Benchley and Dottie remained very close. Brought together by their own insecurities, they were almost inseparable and at one time took an office together above the Metropolitan Opera, where they promised themselves they would work hard. They even arranged for a joint cable address, "Park Bench." Unhappily, this did nothing more than give them privacy for their own conversations, and produced little writing for either. When Benchley went to California to make his movie shorts, Dorothy was so desperate for company that she took the sign off the men's room and planted it on her office door, so that she had a steady stream of "visitors."

I was present at luncheon one afternoon where although Dorothy had imbibed she seemed relatively sober. (We were speaking about a Broadway play about which Heywood Broun, as a critic, had commented "The curtain rose at 8:30 sharp and came down at 10:30 dull." There followed a litany of other verbal murders.) Dottie invited me for cocktails on the next afternoon, explaining that she was having a few friends over.

On my way to keep the rendezvous, I began to have second thoughts. Dottie was, to borrow the title of one of Hitchcock's best pictures, "Notorious." Though sexually interesting to many men, to me she was not. Suppose there were no friends at this cocktail party: just the two of us. If, as I began to worry, she made a pass at me, how would I extricate myself from a potentially awkward situation? Under no circumstances did I wish to jeopardize my occasional access to the Round Tablers, that sparkling array of wits and raconteurs whose unmatched command of the English language and excellence at repartee were a joy to behold. I was happy just to sit quietly at the table — any table — and admire their brilliance. The more I pondered, the more uneasy I became. Not only was Dorothy capable of saying some pretty awful things to conceal an emotional hurt, she said them wonderfully. This was, after all, a woman who upon hearing that Clare Boothe Luce was always kind to her inferiors, remarked, "Where does she find them?"; who responded to a boorish guest's claim that he couldn't bear fools with the line, "That's strange, your mother could"; who on being advised of the fact that Calvin Coolidge had died, asked, "How could they tell?" I had a sudden vision of myself as the target of a particularly devastating Parker epigram, one memorable enough to follow me around from "21" to Wall Street: it was not the kind of immortality I desired.

At the appointed time, I arrived at her hotel — Dottie could not suffer the idea of household chores, and lived for the most part in apartments at the New Weston, the Algonquin, and across the street at the Royalton, explaining to one and all that, as far as she was concerned, "home was just a place to lay her hat and a few friends" — and received a strange look from the maid who asked me to identify myself. I explained that Mrs. Parker had invited me for cocktails. The maid disappeared, only to return in five minutes to inform me that Mrs. Parker had never heard of me. As I stood there, somewhat surprised, Dottie suddenly appeared on the scene and, looking quite puzzled, asked, "Charlie! Did I invite you to cocktails?"

We passed a pleasant and thoroughly innocent afternoon. No man has ever been as pleased as I to discover how far off track his imagination had led him.

More important, I was still eligible to attend the great feast of language that seemed to perpetually surround Dorothy: George S. Kaufman, a world-class bridge player, responding to a clumsy partner's request to be excused to go to the men's room: "My pleasure, because this will be the first time today I know what you have in your hand" ; Dottie just back from Paris complaining that "the crossing had been so rough that the only thing I could keep on my stomach was the first mate"; Kaufman again, responding to a press agent who asked how to get his leading lady's name in George's column — "Shoot her"; Dottie's celebrated gloss on the word "horticulture" — "You can lead a horticulture but you can't make her think."

Elegantly turned phrases from that era still echo in my head. What I can't remember (at age 85) is whether I was indeed present when they were uttered or whether I've absorbed some of them from the countless books I have since read about the protagonists. What I do remember is that conversation with Benchley, Dottie, Aleck Woolcott, GSK, and Heywood Broun was never less than exhilarating and, if I didn't actually hear a particular celebrated retort, I heard something equally delightful.

In those days, I was a good listener—I seem to have lost that skill with age! Now, among family or in my own circle of friends, I tend to hold center court. But should the ghosts of Parker, Benchley, or any of that dazzling, raffish crew return briefly to earth, I would gladly relinquish the floor and again sit contentedly at the edge of the table: no tongue, all eyes and ears.

But the night is still young...

Put on your coat and cruise down 52nd Street between Fifth and Seventh Avenues. Small nightclubs showcase the piano virtuosity of the likes of Art Tatum or the guitar and banjo wizardry of Eddie Condon, and the trumpet of Louis Prima will blare into the wee hours. Tommy Dorsey (who became a lifelong friend of mine), Artie Shaw, and Harry James are playing as side men in smoky little rooms as they sharpen their skills for the great bands of the forties and fifties, including those of Benny Goodman and Glenn Miller. After 2:00 A.M., when the musicians have finished their sets, they will gather for jam sessions at the Famous Door, the Onyx club, or some obscure dusty brownstones; if you know the drummer, you can get inside.

Or grab a cab and go up to Harlem. Even at 2:00 A.M., one can walk the streets without fear. If you love to dance, or to watch wonderful amateur dancers, there is the Savoy Ballroom. And, of course, there's the Cotton Club at 135th Street and Lenox Avenue, presenting such greats as Cab Calloway, Duke Ellington, Eubie Blake, and Lionel Hampton — there is even a sixteen-year-old chorus girl (whom everybody is talking about) by the name of Lena Horne.

Step into Dickie Wells' or Gladys Bentley's or Small's Paradise and you will see people arriving from El Morocco or the Stork Club, resplendent in white tie and tails or dinner jackets, eager to enjoy this different kind of music. There is no visible tension between blacks and whites; racial violence is almost unknown, and any problems which arise are swiftly dealt with by the management — the police are rarely involved. Just settle back and tap your toes to the beat of Lionel Hampton or listen to Billie Holiday or Lee Wylie.

You never know who you might run into at Smalls: your landlady; Mayor Jimmie Walker or his successor, Fiorello LaGuardia; the writer Carl Van Vechten or a broker you made a trade with in the afternoon; maybe even George Gershwin, sitting quietly at a corner table, listening intently to the black American sound he would celebrate in so much of his best work.

I met George Gershwin in 1933. I was squiring Miss Charlene Tucker, a dancer, then in rehearsal for Gershwin's political satire *Let 'Em Eat Cake*, directed by George Kaufman. Her roommate was dating George and, one night, we found ourselves up at his new penthouse on East 72nd Street, listening to the composer of *Rhapsody in Blue* play the piano. It was a modest bachelor apartment of fourteen rooms and contained three pianos: that way he was never very far away from one. He was more comfortable with a piano than with people. When he entered a room full of strangers, he would immediately head for the Steinway. (George S. Kaufman observed that if the race to the piano ever became an Olympic event, Gershwin would beat any other composer by at least three lengths.) A private telephone was connected to Ira Gershwin's apartment across the street. It was the first time that George and Ira Gershwin did not live in the same building.

Gershwin was slim, extremely well-mannered, with a dark complexion which could flood with color; when he was seated at the piano his smile was dazzling. He played through the entire score of *Let 'Em Eat Cake* that evening, something he had evidently been doing in every drawing room in town (Kaufman sourly predicted that by the time the show opened it would be considered a revival). Though it was well known that George favored playing his own music, that night I heard him play everything from Beethoven to Jerome Kern. In the very early morning, as his fingers glided over the keyboard, playing a tumultuous cascade from the *Rhapsody* and shifting to the languor of *The Man I Love*, I stood beside him in the luxurious new penthouse, gazing out the windows at the silent skyscrapers, the moon over the East River, and the stars on the horizon and I thought: "This is a night that should never end."

But, then, I could have said that on any of a thousand New York nights, touched as they were with the wondrous madness of a time that all of us who were lucky enough to experience will never forget.

✧ ✧ ✧

Dawn, alas.

Still floating in a dream, the last bars of music echoing in my head, I would drag myself home.

I have a distinct memory of my brother Bill, worried about my taste for show girls and the high life, waiting in the hall one night to inform me that beauty was only skin deep.

"That's good enough," I replied with a yawn. "Do you think I'm looking for a gall bladder by Michelangelo?"

Somehow, I always made it to work in the morning.

4

WALL STREET IN THE THIRTIES

"Bill," I announced one morning over the phone to my friend Bill Golden at Carl M. Loeb & Co., "I have a date with a terrific girl on Saturday night; but I need to make seventy-five bucks to pay for it. What do you like today?" It was generally my practice, before the opening of the market, to call half a dozen or so of my contemporaries on the Street and chat with them about what they had done the previous night, the sporting news, the most recent statement by FDR, and, of course, what stocks looked particularly interesting. A stock that was in favor, that might move half a dollar, would produce a comfortable day's earnings if you bought four or five hundred shares. Bill thought for a moment and answered, "I can't tell you that it will happen by Friday, but I have just taken four hundred dollars, which is all the money I have in the world, and bought stock in a new company called Climax Molybdenum." Molybdenum was a new word to me and I very cleverly said, "Think of something else. I can't pronounce the word, and if I want to sell it, I may not be able to do so quickly enough." I asked him what price the stock was selling at and he said, "Two dollars." I laughed and sought advice elsewhere.

About two months later, same cast, same question, same answer. I inquired where the stock was now selling and he told me at three and a half. I politely asked him if he was trying to unload it on me, and said I was not about to be victimized.

Much later, I bought the stock at fifteen! When I sold it at twenty-one I decided to call Bill and give him my best advice: "Look, originally I was wrong, but now you're committing financial suicide. You better get out before they send the cops." Bill said that I had made a mistake selling; he was going to stay with it. I knew there was no dealing with stubbornness and I decided to let the fates teach him a lesson.

A couple of years later, I purchased one hundred shares of the same stock at thirty and sold it at thirty-five. I once again offered my best counsel and said, "At least sell half!" He said it was not the right time. In frustration, I asked when he was going to sell. After a moment's reflection Bill replied, "Perhaps at five hundred." When Climax had been split ten to one and was selling at fifty, the equivalent of his five hundred, Bill still had his original position. The wealth generated by that single act of courage allowed him to spend most of his life as an individual investor and a dollar-a-year person in special government service. He was deputy to Admiral Lewis Strauss, chairman of the Atomic Energy Commission. Golden was also, until recently, chairman of the Museum of Natural History.

Since I have no memory at all of the Saturday night date which provoked my initial inquiry, I can only assume that my short term needs were less pressing than they seemed to be at the time. There is a lesson to be drawn here, but I leave it to the reader to do so. In the meantime, should you ever wish to expose my true lack of insight into the market, you need only say the word "molybdenum" — if you can pronounce it!

1933 and 1934 were tough business years. We were in a depression, people were not starting new ventures, jobs were scarce, and in our small brokerage firm we lived from one day to another. In the early days of 1935, when we were wondering if the stock ticker would ever move, I received a call from my friend Sylvan Coleman at E. F. Hutton. He directed me to get to his office post haste, and inferred that my hour had struck.

Sylvan was a new breed of employee at the silk-stocking firm of E. F. Hutton. He did not spring from the Ivy League colleges, with the manipulative hand of a father or an uncle easing his way through the canyons of Wall Street. He had come from the University of Southern California and Harvard Business School in 1931, with nothing to recommend him except his extraordinary brilliance. His rise at E. F. Hutton was meteoric. In a move that, for those days, was equivalent to the result of a visit to Lourdes, he became the first partner at Hutton who did not contribute one million dollars in capital, largely because he did not have a million dollars. Ed Hutton and Ruloff Cutten began to turn over to Sylvan the management of some of the major house accounts involving presidents or chairmen of some of the great American corporations and famous society figures. Sylvan had occasionally used me as Hutton's representative in moderate transactions, and I had managed to avoid calamity. I eagerly set off for my appointment with my fingers crossed, thinking to myself: "Between being good and being lucky, give me lucky every time."

Upon my arrival at 61 Broadway, I was ushered into a room where sat the Grand Vizier of E. F. Hutton with his court attendants, Ruloff Cutten and Sylvan Coleman. A rather strange-looking man, who apparently dyed his hair red, was also present. His appearance was that of a hired hand who needed a new tailor.

Right on cue Ed Hutton said, "Charles, I would like you to meet Paul Getty." I caught my breath and listened. Getty was a renowned interloper, an independent oil discoverer who literally walked around the desert in flowing Arab costume. The monopolists in the industry hated his maverick approach. It now developed that Mr. Getty was intent on gaining control of a particular oil company, but if he was identified as the buyer in any stock transaction, there would be unwelcome followers buying the stock as well.

Since much of Paul Getty's business at that time was handled by E. F. Hutton & Co., using them as a broker for this purpose was a sure tip-off. In an attempt to avoid creating a bull market in the stock, they decided that the best procedure was to find an anonymous young man who had no possible connection with J. Paul Getty. The job description, additionally, called for somebody who was a good broker, and competent enough to conceal his hand.

Another requisite was that the broker would act solely on behalf of Getty, and not be tempted into buying stock for "his cousins and his uncles and his aunts." Given the manner in which Wall Street inmates had comported themselves in the past, this substantially narrowed the field. Swayed by the strong recommendation of my friend Sylvan, and the manner in which

I had handled previous transactions, Hutton had decided to present me as a candidate.

I was being interviewed for something which was of a magnitude beyond my comprehension. During those very difficult days, an order for five hundred shares of stock was welcome, one thousand shares a bonanza, and two thousand shares called for a celebration.

Paul Getty looked at me for a moment, and said, "Young man, if I give you an order to buy one million shares of stock, how many shares will you buy for yourself first?" I looked helplessly from one person to another, and everybody nodded in a friendly way that assured me I wasn't talking to a nut. I replied, "Mr. Getty, in my family, we work every week to feed and clothe ourselves. We have no money to allocate for investments. In answer to your question, I can only represent one person on any deal at a time, and I would be pleased if it were you."

Getty said, "All right. I would like you to buy one million shares of Mission Corporation, which is traded over the counter, at the market price. Moreover, I ask you that, although the price is currently around eight-and-a-half dollars, you must never refuse an offer of a thousand shares at even twelve dollars a share or more."

When I heard these words, I changed feet because if ever there was a way to murder a transaction in the marketplace, he had given me the weapon. This was also a lifetime opportunity with commissions in six figures. I needed to respond carefully to this request, lest he summon the gendarmes. It would take a bravura performance. I spoke thusly: "Mr. Getty, from all I have read or heard, you are the quintessential finder of oil. You know that business perhaps as well as anyone else, but the rules that apply in the oil business are not necessarily applicable to the job at hand.

"If I were to proceed as directed, when I finally finished the job, you would have paid a good deal more than what is possible by careful, sensible management of the order. Worse, I would have ended what I hope will be an enduring relationship. So I think you are going to have to decide whether you'd like to manage the purchases of this stock, or whether you are satisfied that I am, at least in this environment, more skilled than you are."

Warming to my subject, I continued, "Good brokers sometimes do things to misdirect the sharks." I explained that it was possible to be a buyer of stock and yet confuse the opposition by selling shares from time to time, so that others might find it difficult to identify the kind of mischief that was occupying your time. Obviously, one would buy far more than he sold, but he might make a lot more noise in the transactions on the sell side so that they would attract attention. This would be a red herring, but properly introduced, its pungent aroma would divert a pack of hounds from their proper quarry. Unless I was able to do this, each time I made a phone call everybody would be alert to the fact that I was a buyer of shares.

I added, "This is the first time I have ever been offered such an opportunity. I want this order, but not if I am doomed to certain failure. I am confident that I can do the job, but we can't have two chiefs." (This practice of buying and selling, legal at that time, was later frowned upon by the SEC and is no longer permitted. This leads to the inevitable conclusion that bureaucrats want to reduce citizens to robots and that the use of brains or imagination gives one citizen too great an advantage over another.)

Getty replied, "All right, you provide me with that result in the way that you consider the most effective, and when you have finished with this million shares, I will give you an order for as much as required." After comforting glances from Ruloff Cutten and Ed Hutton that assured me that I was not in an asylum, my feet barely touched the ground en route to my office.

Bursting in the door, I sang out the news. Instead of enthusiasm, however, my partners went into catatonic shock.

They needlessly explained to me that, given our modest capital beyond the value of our seat on the Curb Exchange, if Mr. Getty ever refused a report or took off for Shangri-La, we would be bankrupt in the blink of an eye. I didn't need that intelligence. When the noise had settled down, terror was in the air. I delivered my ultimatum, "Listen, Sylvan is my best friend, and he is not a moron. If you are lucky just once in your lifetime, you may have an opportunity to make it big. I believe this is mine. In fact, it is ours, and unless we are prepared to take this order and execute it promptly, the partnership is over this goddamn minute. I have no intention of standing on a street corner and waiting around for another miracle."

A dissolved partnership was not a consummation devoutly to be wished by my partners. After some hysterical moments, they announced that if they could go upstairs and discuss this with good old Uncle Joe, they would bet their lives, provided Uncle Joe approved.

I patiently explained to them that Paul Getty and Ed Hutton were doing me the greatest kindness that I had yet experienced in the business world, and that I was not about to expose their hand to a competitor. It was all or none. They caved in, but the room was redolent with the aroma and hush of Campbell's funeral parlor.

I will not dazzle you with the imaginative manner in which I assisted Mr. Getty in making his fortune, nor will I relate the utter confusion that I engendered in the marketplace, causing everybody to wonder whether I was a buyer or a seller. The fact is that it was not that difficult. After a few months, we proceeded on the second million shares. We missed several opportunities for immense transactions because of the unwillingness of my partners to buy, even for a ten-minute period, a large block of stock above market price, for fear of Getty's refusal to accept the report.

He was genuinely pleased with our performance. The substantial commissions gave us for the first time some financial strength, which we hoped could be the foundation for future growth. Parenthetically, I paid my debts to my friends at "21" and to Daxe the tailor. I could now face the world with the serene countenance of a man who owned his pants.

There was only one occasion on which I regretted Getty visiting me. In the 1950s I was on the floor of the New York Stock Exchange during the trading day, and one of the security guards brought me Paul's business card. With a strange look he said, "He's out there waiting." I assumed that he was impressed with the fact that such an important man would come to visit me on the floor. I was soon disabused.

I mentioned earlier that, upon meeting Paul, I had noted that he dyed his hair red, but I've seen ladies who dye their hair blue. Unknown to me, however, was the fact that there is sometimes a chemical reaction in these dyes, by which rather strange and wonderful results are achieved. Being bald, there was no reason for me to familiarize myself with these problems. I went out to meet Getty, and was tempted to turn tail and run. His hair had turned a Kelly green. Needless to say, he was the cynosure of all eyes in the lobby of the Stock Exchange building. We greeted one another and he said that he had never met a specialist in his stock and would like to do so now.

For a moment I panicked, because the Stock Exchange floor was filled with fun-loving, unpredictable clowns. The specialist in Getty Oil, Robert Jacobson, was one of my good friends, so

I suggested to Paul that it might be a better idea if we all met in my office so that he would have the comfort and leisure to discuss matters with his floor representative. He declined this offer, and I was now faced with the dismaying prospect of walking across the Exchange floor to the farthest point from our present location in order to reach the post at which Getty Oil was traded. I can only equate that walk with the same exhilarating feeling one must have enjoyed riding in a tumbrel, or on a stroll from a prison cell to the electric chair. It was several months before the comedians ceased standing in front of me during slow periods, wearing green fright wigs to remind me of that joyful day.

In later years, Getty occupied an enormous English estate with numerous rooms and servants, yet it is a fact that he installed a pay phone. I don't know why, except that he may have invited people who made calls to Outer Mongolia. This did not change my opinion of his generosity.

Paul Getty and I remained friends until his demise. I found him to be very fair and for many years, even while he was living in England, we had similarly satisfactory dealings. There was, moreover, some happy fallout from the time when Getty announced the acquisition of Mission Corporation. I was immediately identified as a player in that game and was brought to the attention of Bernard Baruch.

While Getty was a very determined and strong-willed negotiator, he suffered from a delusion common since the beginning of time. In matters related to the distaff side, he had a fine eye, but the extraordinary notion that this was just like business. He convinced himself that it was his ineffable charm that brought the ladies to his side, a misconception that tumbled empires, undid Samson and Mark Antony, and added a Trojan horse to the animal kingdom.

Among Paul's many less-than-steamy romances was a frolic with a thrush named Miss Teddy Lynch who plied her trade at the Stork Club. It was a cinch that since her voice was rather thin, it was her charms of a more visible and imposing nature that hypnotized Paul into surrendering to matrimony. It was less a marriage of May and September than of February and December. With an unerring instinct, Getty chose the time just prior to the Second World War for his wedding; no political prognosticator, the former songstress was soon en route for a holiday in Italy. She was trapped there for the duration, so their association could hardly be defined as drenched in passion.

The new Mrs. Getty could not be classed with Rosemary Clooney or Dinah Shore, but with the help of Mr. Getty's bankroll she cut a number of records. Sylvan Coleman was making his first trip to Europe as a partner of E. F. Hutton. He had just settled himself in his cabin on the ship when the purser arrived, bearing a note and a receipt for a packing case. Sylvan innocently inquired, "What kind of a packing case?" The purser responded, "Large and heavy." After scanning the note, Sylvan was choleric, for he was apprised that Mr. Getty had generously granted to Mr. Sylvan Coleman the great honor of acting as Miss Teddy Lynch's representative in London. Enclosed therewith was a plea from Paul that Sylvan visit the Gramophone Shop in London to see if he could peddle the records there.

Sylvan turned menacingly to the purser and said, "Dump the damn thing overboard." It is possible therefore to say that Teddy Lynch's chanteys are secure, with treasures from Spanish galleons and ancient Athens, in Davy Jones' locker.

✧ ✧ ✧

After the finalization of the purchase of Mission Corporation in 1936, I was informed by Arthur Newmark, a partner in a firm headed by Bernard Baruch's brother, that Barney Baruch would like to speak with me. That exciting and promising news made my heart quicken, and a week later I was ushered into the presence of the man himself. At sixty-five years of age he was still a most imposing, elegant, and distinguished gent. Tall and courtly, he effused a honeyed southern charm, but his piercing eyes, though bespectacled, were laser-sharp.

My host was curious about the Mission acquisition for Getty, and he seemed to approve of the manner in which we had concealed our hand. He understood the feints which aided the achievement of our objective. He quizzed me closely about myself, with questions which were direct, never casual, and by the time he was finished, he could have written my biography. I found the experience very exhilarating. I left not really knowing why he had called me, but I was certain that I would hear from him.

Bernard Baruch was arguably the most famous venture capitalist and trader in the stock market ever to appear on the American scene. More than a financier, Baruch had risen to prominence during World War One as an advisor to President Wilson; later he became a confidante of FDR. He was a trusted friend to many European statesmen and won civic awards in Belgium, Italy, and France, as well as the Distinguished Service Medal in the US. Word has it that Barney made profitable investments for Winston Churchill, which may not have been enough to make him wealthy, but which certainly kept the British bulldog in brandy and cigars.

Contrary to some of the extravagant statements made retrospectively, Baruch actually was not short the market in either 1927 or 1929, when the crashes came. Later, he developed a trading philosophy which he followed religiously. It could be summed up in four words: "In general, run quickly." In spite of the substantial setback in 1929, by the end of 1930, according to his biographer, James Grant, Baruch owned $3,691,874.00 in stocks, $3,067,465.00 in bonds, and $8,698,000 in cash. This total of more than $15 million was, as Damon Runyon would have put it, "more than somewhat."

As a souvenir, Barney's secretary, Mrs. Boyle, had also un-covered 114,000 shares of Baltimore & Ohio Railroad stock (of which Barney was a director) with a market value of zero. Baruch understood that there is no law which says you must make back the money that you lost on the same stock. Some-times he just decided he was wrong. He would ask himself the question: "If I did not own it, would I buy it today?" If the an-swer was "No," he would sell.

In the mid-1930s, Baruch had completely reversed his posi-tion and was playing the short side of the market. He wrote a memo to himself, outlining the disciplines by which he pro-posed to operate. They were constantly before him:

SELF-RELIANCE: Do your own thinking. Don't let your emotions enter into it. Keep out of any environment that may affect your acting on your reason.

JUDGMENT: Consider all the facts — meditate on them. Don't let what you want to happen influence your judg-ment.

COURAGE: Don't overestimate the courage you will need if things go against you.

ALERTNESS: To discover any new facts that change the situ-ation, or which may affect public opinion.

PRUDENCE: Be pliable or you won't be prudent. Become more humble as the market goes your way. It is not prudent to buy when you think the bottom has been reached. It is better to wait and see, and buy too late. It is not prudent to wait for the top of the market to sell — it is better to sell "too soon." (Never buy so that your margin will be less than 85%, or hold if it drops below 80%. In a particularly "clear sky" situation with[out] "buts" or "ifs," one can lower these margins to 80%-75%.)

PLIABILITY: Consider and reconsider the facts and your opinions. Stubbornness as to opinions — "cockiness" — must be entirely eliminated. A determination to make a certain amount within a certain time absolutely destroys pliability. When you decide, act promptly — don't wait to see what the market will do.

For my own purpose, I have added another maxim made a few years ago by Norman Augustine, chairman of Martin Marietta. It appeals to me as an insurance policy calculated to keep you out of the poor house:

GREAT EXPECTATIONS:
About ninety percent of the time, things will turn out worse than you expect, and the other ten percent of the time, you had no right to expect so much.

Baruch had some failures, certainly, but he developed the habit of going somewhere alone, perhaps to a park bench, or for a few days to his parents' residence in Long Branch, New Jersey, to analyze what had gone wrong.

He became a governor of the New York Stock Exchange and was even accepted by J. P. Morgan, which was quite extraordinary, since J. P. Morgan rarely had relationships with Jews.

One of Baruch's maternal ancestors, Isaac Rodriguez Marques, a Spanish-Portuguese ship owner, landed in New York in 1690. Subsequently the family moved to Camden, South Carolina. In 1800, when Barney's grandmother settled in New York, she Americanized their name to Marks.

His father, Dr. Simon Baruch, left Prussia in 1840 in order to avoid compulsory military service. Ironically, a few years after his arrival in this country, the Civil War erupted and he volunteered to serve in the Confederate Army. Having attended a junior medical college, he was commissioned as an assistant surgeon, and served throughout the war. He was actually captured twice, but was released. He went on to become a respected Professor of Medicine at Columbia University. When he died, his Confederate uniform was folded and placed in the casket with him.

It was curious that, even though Barney resided in New York most of his life, he never lost his southern accent. It set him apart. In the last analysis, I suppose, he was a great actor.

In the late fifties, when Baruch was eighty-eight years old, my wife and I had dinner with him and his nurse. I suggested that he had been the most successful speculator spanning three generations and inquired whether he harbored any specific regrets. He thought for a moment and said, "I sold too soon."

Baruch's great success began when he was entrusted with several missions by the great Thomas Fortune Ryan, and he later became a key player in the battle with E. H. Harriman for control of the Union Pacific. In fact, the peace pact finally settled upon was conceived in large measure by Baruch. The railroad success was followed by many others on behalf of the Ryan group. Not only did it bring Baruch to the forefront of the major players, but it became the foundation for the success of A. A. Housman & Co., in which firm Baruch was a partner.

In retrospect, what Baruch did for Thomas Fortune Ryan and associates paralleled what I had been asked to do for Paul Getty and subsequently for Baruch himself. I have no suspicion that I acquitted myself as nobly as Baruch did in his twenties, but my affiliation with him taught me that in no other business does fame by association flourish as it does on Wall Street. I deluded myself into believing I had become a full member of the Establishment.

I was soon called by Mr. Baruch to handle orders for him and some of his associates. (He was referred to as BMB by some friends, as the Governor by others, but I always called him Mr. Baruch.) Baruch was a great advocate of confining your investment activities to those industries you best understood. He often chided me that my own firm was dealing with more unrelated industries than could be adequately understood. He would then smile and express his own low opinion of the advice that was offered in the financial community. "You can generally copper it," he grinned. "You'll make a lot of money that way."

Less than two weeks after my original meeting with Mr. Baruch, he contacted me to discuss his proposed purchase of a large block of a mining stock. He had joined with a senator from Nevada to buy Gold Field Consolidated Mining, whose properties adjoined a company called Combination Mines, owned by the senator.

The proposal offered by Baruch involved a complex exchange of shares of Gold Field and a relatively small amount of cash for Combination Mine owners. The more stock, the less cash. In order for the transaction to be a big winner, it was essential that Gold Field Consolidated remain very steady on the New York Curb. Baruch reasoned that one of the other partners of Combination Mines, on hearing of the proposed exchange of shares, would think that he could manage a financial coup by selling Consolidated heavily on the New York Curb. He would be driving the price up to a level that made the exchange much more favorable to Combination Mines shareholders.

BMB anticipated just such a ploy, and he decided that he would place buy orders and hold the stock on the Curb Exchange to within a small fraction of its present value. That is where I came in. In addition to myself, he had one or two brokers operating on his behalf in a smaller way, while I was quiescent in order to confuse the opposition into thinking that the purchasing was broad-based.

He entered an order with me to buy Gold Field, anticipating a large sell order from the other side. This guess proved prescient and displayed a strength of Gold Field stock that completely undid the sellers. The rock-solid performance of Gold Field shares, even faced with large-scale selling, persuaded the largest stockholders of Combination Mines to accept Consolidated stock, for the most part, in lieu of cash. Baruch and the senator gained control.

As opposed to my relationship with Getty, wherein I was fundamentally the decision maker on the manner in which the order should be executed, Baruch had calculated strategy down to the smallest detail.

It became the custom, after a day on the floor of the Exchange, for me to meet with Mr. Baruch in his office overlooking Trinity Church. I reported events in the most careful detail, even the personal reactions of the brokers on the floor. He had a great interest in how the market had reacted during these procedures. When he commented, I listened intently and found that my education was furthered. Through his eyes, I began to see the marketplace in its simplest, most uncomplicated form.

At one session, he recounted the philosophy of Sir Ernest Cassell, the private banker to King Edward VI. When Cassell was young and began to enjoy some success, he was labeled a gambler who should be watched as possibly unreliable. As his business affairs expanded in scope and in size, he was looked upon as a speculator. When the universe of his transactions continued to grow, he was soon known as a banker. "The truth is," said Mr. Baruch, "he was doing the same thing all the time."

If you harbored the notion that there was such a thing as a sure investment, you were headed for the poor house. "J. P. Morgan," he said, "could look upon me as gambler and gag when I used the word. Nevertheless, there is no investment that does not involve some risk and therefore, by definition, is a gamble of some kind."

The most successful people try to reduce the element of risk. You must not make an ass of yourself by overestimating your cunning or betting the farm on one venture. At other times, he confirmed my conviction that the true speculator acts on information and belief, estimates the future, tests his answer, including the result of a misjudgment, and then acts. He underlined the need to re-evaluate your judgment unemotionally from time to time and to be realistic, to get out promptly if your judgment proved wrong. Act skillfully and with surgical precision. Once you have made up your mind, don't dawdle; transact.

Baruch believed that the real problem people had was their difficulty in disentangling themselves from their own emotions. The actuator that drives stocks up or down is not impersonal economic factors or changing events, but the human reaction to these events.

He would emphasize to me that in no field is the venerable maxim "a little knowledge is a dangerous thing" more valid than in investing. His conviction was that the most powerful force that starts an economy upward is the simple fact that all of us must find a way to live.

As a young man just graduated from City College, Barney Baruch was addicted to body building, and attracted admiration from the ladies. He frequented a gymnasium on 28th Street whose habitués were lawyers, brokers, merchants, and prize-fighters. Among them was Bob Fitzsimmons, onetime heavy-weight champion of the world, who told Barney that he didn't hit hard enough, and offered the following useful advice: "When you hit a man in the jaw, try to knock his block off. When you hit him in the belly, try to drive your glove clean through him." He further enjoined, "Don't get mad when you are fighting." Baruch applied that last bit of advice in business dealings: "If you are angry, you are not thinking," he said.

Baruch engaged in a number of bouts at the gym, one of them against a policeman whose beat was along Fifth Avenue. The early rounds saw the City College boy taking an awful pasting, but the policeman got momentarily careless. With every ounce of energy he had, Baruch hit him with a jarring left to the stomach and followed it with a crunching right to the jaw. The lawman crashed to the canvas, where he had to be revived by a bucket of water. Baruch always remained a boxing fan and kept himself in excellent physical shape.

Attracted to the theater in general, and to the ladies in particular, Barney tried to further his brother Hartwig's theatrical ambitions. Earning only five dollars a week at the time, Baruch canvassed all of his friends and raised enough to finance Harty and an actress friend.

During the First World War, Barney was chairman of the War Industries Board, and President Wilson astonished him by teasing him about the episode. Baruch wondered how Wilson knew of this escapade, until the President laughingly told him that John Golden, the theatrical producer, had related the tale of what he described as "Barney Baruch's dramatic exit, if not spectacular entrance, as a theatrical producer."

Hartwig had been studying at a dramatic school, where he

was smitten by a beautiful older woman, whom he naturally believed to be a great talent. He was aflame with visions of the bright future that awaited them both. All they needed was someone to back *East Lynne*, the show which they proposed to do. Barney immediately stepped into the breach with the money he had collected. *East Lynne* was a staple potboiler in all touring troupes, and everyone assumed that everyone else knew their lines, thus obviating the need for prolonged and tedious rehearsals.

When the curtain rose on a lovely spring evening in Centerville, New Jersey, the audience filled a meager three rows. The first act was an unmitigated disaster. Most of the actors had only a passing acquaintance with their lines, and the audience's reactions alternated from outraged (the investors) to mildly amused (the investors' guests). During Act Two, the only discernible emotion was anger. Since the audience outnumbered the performers, Baruch requested that the box office return the money to the paying patrons. The cast was spirited out of the stage door and was probably at the railroad station before the audience realized there would be no third act. Despite this rather dismal introduction, Baruch maintained his love of the theater.

Barney also loved his large estate in South Carolina, which was named Hobcaw. He enjoyed hunting and entertained people there from all over the world.

He once described to me the weekend guest who had long proclaimed his love of hunting and boasted of his accuracy with a gun. One morning, a small party went out on a turkey shoot, and it developed that the guest was no rival to Annie Oakley. A second day of frenetic efforts netted this gent exactly no birds.

Suddenly, on the third and very desperate day of his quest, he spotted a particularly fine gobbler, motionless on the branch of a tree. Silently he crept up and, taking careful aim, fired at point-blank range. The bird fell at his feet. With a sigh of triumphant relief, he picked up his kill and began to stuff it in his bag when he noticed a discreet card attached to the bird. It read, "With the compliments of Bernard M. Baruch."

Fortunately for me, my association with Baruch became known to key players, and while the market and the economy were not then conducive to making millions in commissions, the coupling of my name with his provided a certain stature to our firm. It brought us new and interesting clients, who reasoned that if Baruch had found us useful, we might also add something to their cause.

One of the most valuable things I learned from Barney (something that is still not widely understood), is that all money ultimately goes back to the people. Great wealth almost always equates to great philanthropy. Carnegie, Morgan, Mellon, Ford, Frick, Astor, Rockefeller, Getty, Stanford, Harkness, and Duke, who have been whipping boys for nobodies, have endowed the great museums, libraries, and symphony orchestras. In fact, J. P. Morgan had spent his entire fortune on Egyptian art and the splendid library on Madison Avenue which bears his name. Upon his death in Rome, his remarkable collection of antiquities was left to the Metropolitan Museum of Art.

Barney Baruch also did one thing which had a notable effect on my life many years later, although no thought of that even entered my mind at the time. He introduced me in 1939 to Billy Rose, née Rosenberg, the producer, impresario, and theater personality. Billy had been Barney's secretary during his Washington years with the Wilson Administration.

At the time of the outbreak of the First World War, a man named Gregg had developed a new method of speed writing that was of enormous use to secretaries in businesses throughout the land. It was called shorthand. At a time when there were no dictation machines and word processors, this would become a tremendous boon to the burgeoning business environment. Gregg's problem was how to bring this spectacular break-through to the attention of the general public. With very little money, he began to give free lessons in the public schools and arranged for good students be rewarded in some fashion. One such student was William Rosenberg, and Gregg took Billy across the country to give shorthand exhibitions.

Although America did not enter the war for almost three years, it was soon apparent that the time was approaching to marshal resources. President Wilson appointed Barney to ac-complish that goal, and Baruch realized the growing necessity for an efficient method of communication. He contacted Gregg and asked who the best shorthand writer in America was at the time. Without a moment's hesitation Gregg said, "A fifteen year-old boy in the Bronx, by the name of William Rosenberg."

A short time thereafter, William Rosenberg was living at the White House with Barney Baruch, and a career that would pro-pel a young man from a tenement to a palace was on its way.

Charles & Marie McDonald, circa 1940

5

HOLLYWOOD

The financial markets remained in a somnolent state throughout the 1930s. There would be moments when optimism raised its uncertain head, but they were scattered and unconvincing. Our small firm did manage to make some minor progress each year, and though we were not knocking down any fences, we always had work. But it was no longer an adventure, no longer a challenge. It seemed I was just sitting at my desk, talking on the phone, buying and selling stocks; my career had turned into a job.

I began to fear that I had taken a giant step towards a life in the suburbs. If you are a lathe operator, you just do the job; if you are a stock analyst, it may take a year of waiting to see a result. I couldn't wait for another miracle like Getty. There were other worlds to conquer, undertakings that would engage my imagination and keep my spirits soaring. The urge to try my hand at something new began to haunt me night and day, but in taking inventory, it became obvious that I had no extraordinary skills outside the financial arena. I began to regret the time I had spent playing handball while at college.

Motion pictures were still in their adolescence, and fame and fortune were in Hollywood waiting to be plucked. But in what capacity would I pluck them? Although I had once read an essay by the great Russian *cinéaste* Sergei Eisenstein and had seen all the pictures of John Ford, none of my talents at golf, tennis, or squash qualified me as a likely replacement for either of them. My experience as an actor in an amateur theatrical group did not suggest to anyone that I was "star material." It was clear, then, that my most promising entry level position would have to be achieved by writing the Great American Picture Show.

I had, after all, actually done some writing. Having been, in my opinion, unjustifiably punished as an adolescent for some slight infraction of the house rules, I wrote my mother a note presenting my viewpoint. She was intrigued by this approach and encouraged me to always write down what I did not feel able to say directly, a practice I continued until I was nineteen. In addition, our family dinners gave each of us the opportunity to concoct outrageous stories (and wasn't that in essence what Hollywood was about?). The more I thought about it, the more I was convinced that I had undergone the necessary literary apprenticeship: success seemed a foregone conclusion.

On a Monday morning in early 1938, I innocently inquired of my two partners the date of our last meeting. They informed me that it had been the previous Wednesday. I corrected them by announcing we were even now engaged in our last partners' meeting, and that I was heeding the advice of Horace Greeley and going West. They tried desperately to persuade me that, in times like these, one foot on first base was a hell of a lot better than selling apples outside the stadium. I think my friends and colleagues on Wall Street tried to discourage me because they

CHARLES WOHLSTETTER ✑ 77

secretly wished to make such a radical change themselves. I was adamant; Hollywood was going to embrace me whether it was prepared to or not.

A month later, in February, I set my sights for the West, zeroing in on Hollywood, La La Land, where the lotus was the flower of choice. There I arrived, early one morning, depositing my body and worldly possessions in a rather nice one-room apartment just off Hollywood Boulevard, a short block from Sid Grauman's elaborately gilded Chinese Theater.

It turned out that I was an oddity in the tenant roster. Of the forty-four apartments, forty were occupied by young female fugitives from Idaho, Washington, Texas, Virginia, and other faraway places, who waited patiently by the telephone to hear from Central Casting. Apart from a married character actor, Stanley Ridges, I was the only male resident. It was Shangri-La.

After settling in, I called my friend Felix Feist at MGM Studios. Felix's father had headed the Leo Feist Music Company, which had been merged into Metro, and with his father's clout, Felix had made a solid entry into the motion picture industry. He began as a cameraman before becoming a director of short subjects, particularly Robert Benchley's smash hits, *The Treasurer's Report*, *How to Carve a Turkey*, and *How to Sleep*, which won an Academy Award in 1935. The famous *Pete Smith Specialties* shorts were directed by Felix and are still-unparalleled classics. (Felix Feist's luck failed him only once, but it was in a monumental fashion. He was asked to screen-test Deanna Durbin and Judy Garland for the MGM stock company; he selected Deanna Durbin. The studio signed them both anyway, and Felix redeemed himself by ably directing the two young stars in their first film, *Every Sunday*, in 1936.)

I had frequent opportunities to enjoy Benchley's unique talent on the set. Bob was a mischievous elf and he avoided work with the utmost seriousness. He did not have a malicious bone in his body, however, and was widely loved in Hollywood. I witnessed the filming of one scene which required that he be strung up in a mess of telephone wires above the street. While waiting for Felix to roll the cameras, Benchley asked his wife, Ruth, "Remember how good I was at Latin at Harvard? Well, look where it got me."

Oddly enough, Benchley always thought himself a failure and little more than a lightweight joke writer. He summed up his career thus: "It took me fifteen years to find out that I had no talent for writing, but I couldn't give it up, because by that time, I was too famous." He felt an enormous insecurity, a sense of loss, that he was unable to express himself in the way that he had optimistically thought he would when he first became a scribe. By that time in his life he was, sadly, a hopeless drunk.

I began to spend time on the set, watching how a movie was made. Felix did the pictures involving Howard Hill, the world's greatest archer, who doubled for Errol Flynn in *Robin Hood* and actually split the arrow already embedded in the target in that film. Felix himself was an extraordinary athlete, with enough natural luck to make a living in Las Vegas. During the filming of one picture, Hill was supposed to pull a hundred-pound bow and fire it through an aperture in some battlements about one hundred yards away. He unsuccessfully tried the shot twenty times, until Felix impatiently grabbed the bow and said "My God, what's so difficult about this?" Only half-looking, he fired an arrow which was right on the mark. I am confident that he had not pulled a bow since the age of four, but that was Felix.

On another occasion, Felix and I were playing golf and we came to a par three, 225 yard hole; there was a bank at the back of the green and a wicked bunker right in front of it. I took a wood to my tee-shot, but Felix used a three iron. When we got to the green there was only one ball — mine. We looked in the bunker, up the bank, in the trees, but there was no sign of Felix's ball. A groundskeeper was nearby and we asked him if he had seen a ball come into the vicinity; he smiled and pointed at the cup. Sure enough, there was Felix's ball: a hole-in-one!

I think there is a signal lesson in Felix's shot: even with knowledge and careful study, luck is a required component of success. It also helps if the other guy makes a mistake! Sadly, Felix was not lucky in other ways; when he was only fifty-nine, he died a painful death from cancer.

At The Gourmet, a favorite restaurant on Sunset Boulevard, I was struck by the sight of Virginia Bruce, the beautiful star of *Jane Eyre*, eating lunch alone. I was tongue-tied at the prospect of speaking to her but Felix, to my amazement, walked over to her table and said, "Ginny, how come you're eating alone?" Miss Bruce laughed and replied, "Are you kidding? I haven't had a date in a month." Felix explained to me that only the film industry was flourishing (the great oil, aerospace, and electronics companies were still to come); as a consequence, there were very few young men, and most of them suffered from self-enthrallment. I hasten to add that I was not bold enough to ask Miss Bruce for a date; how history might have changed if I had, we can only wonder. I did, however, rekindle a friendship with one of my East Coast pals, Joan Mitchell. Joan had been a dancer in a New York saloon owned by Barbara Walters' father. She was now a starlet for Metro and was at the studio school with, among others, Lana Turner. Joan said, "Listen, kiddo, I have my own boyfriend, but I am going to introduce you to a candy store." I remember thinking, "I'm going to like this place!"

Eager to begin my first screenwriting skirmish, I explained the germ of a story to Felix. On the train from New York I had hit upon a tale about a young man who was drawn into a confidence scheme by the shady operators of the hotel where he lived. It was speculatively entitled *What Millionaire Playboy*. Felix liked what he heard and told me that he was going to put me in touch with a writer by the name of Syd Zelinka. He had written some radio shows for Jack Oakie, a modest star of the times, and Felix thought Syd's strength was in writing sparkling dialogue but expressed some doubts about his ability to carry a story line. He suggested that we meet the next day on the golf course.

As we played the first few holes, I outlined the springboard of my story to Syd, and on the fourth hole, he suggested we quit and go home and write it. We set about our collaboration in my apartment. Weeks passed as we struggled with syntax. Syd, obviously pleased with his career, would remove the pipe from his mouth and say, "Isn't this a great way to make a living?" Up to that point, we had not seen a dime and I thought we should wait a while before we accepted any Academy Awards, at least until we had either finished the first couple of pages, or until I could pay the rent.

Eventually our story was re-written (in typical Hollywood fashion) and re-titled, though I admit I have forgotten what it was called. Syd and I received a modest fee to split between us for our efforts. Seeing that story produced was not how I had envisioned the glamour of stardom. The process of movie-making is unrelievedly tedious: there would be hours of set-up, a few minutes of filming, then hours more for the next set-up. My visions of the swooping cameras and gliding artsy shots were rapidly dispelled by the grinding monotony of nuts-and-bolts filmmaking.

The product of my labors with Syd was three screenplays, which blessedly have been lost in time. We actually sold two of them, one of which came back to haunt me recently. One sleepless night about five years ago, I turned on the television, and there, to my amazement, was a terrible version of one of our efforts. I did not see the beginning of the film so I don't know who was responsible for it, but I was grateful it was on at three o'clock in the morning because it was a god-awful picture!

Syd was born in the Bronx and, as he recounted it, his father was in the fur business. He dealt not in sable or mink but in dyed rabbit. Like most fathers, Mr. Zelinka foresaw a great future for his son in the family business, a thought which nauseated Syd, who couldn't even look at a bunny on Easter.

After several reluctant attempts at shearing rabbits, Syd grasped the nettle and announced at dinner one night that he intended to be one of the great comic writers and bring fame and fortune to the family. His father looked dubious and his mother burst into tears. Syd had been a very amusing son, but she simply didn't believe that anybody would pay someone for writing jokes. Syd was adamant, and he unsuccessfully set forth to break down the doors of radio producers and theater managers before heading for California. He was eking out a living when we met through Felix.

Syd dutifully called home every couple of weeks to report to the family that his respiratory organs were still functioning and he was eating regularly. He created wonderful stories about the glamour and excitement of his new home, until his mother asked where he was working. Syd would reply, "Mom, I'm writing." As if he had avoided the question, she would ask, "Yes, but what are you doing for a living?" It took many years for Syd to convince his mother that he was not en route to the hoosegow for stealing money.

Jack Benny's radio show was Mrs. Zelinka's favorite, and when it became a television show, she never missed a performance. Somehow or other Mrs. Zelinka did not associate Syd's name on the screen as a writer with being paid real money. Once, Syd arranged for his mother to be at "The Jack Benny Show," and later join Jack and Mary Benny at a popular restaurant called Reuben's.

During the course of the meal, Syd's mother leaned over to Benny and asked in a confidential tone, "Mr. Benny, how is my boy doing?" He nearly fell from his chair, screaming with laughter. In 1945, Benny was paying Syd $3,000 a week. After that evening, Syd was accepted back into the family fold as an honest man making an honest living.

Jack Benny was one of the most respected people in Hollywood, and had the inner security to laugh at himself. One evening, in the 1960s, my wife and I were having dinner in Palm Springs at Ruby's Dunes, and at a nearby table sat Jack and Mary Benny and Kirk and Anne Douglas. As we left the restaurant, we stopped to exchange pleasantries, and Jack invited us to stop by 31 Flavors with him for some ice cream. We were standing on line when a tiny, elderly lady squinted at Jack Benny and inquired in a rather heavy accent, "Is it true that you are Jack Benny?" Benny modestly admitted that he was. The lady shrugged her shoulders and said, "Well, good luck anyway," and walked away. Benny laughed at that for days.

When Syd wrote for the Gleason and Berle shows, my name

turned up in the show as Professor Wohlstetter, the great German scientist, or as Dr. Wohlstetter, the demented dentist. Occasionally I was Charlie, the famous football player from Brazil. They weren't doing this to flatter; this was a tease because I was a friend. Part of the gag was that I always dressed with some care, so in every case both Gleason and Berle showed the character with insane hairstyles, wearing baggy trousers and coats that didn't fit. These episodes still appear on late night reruns.

Gleason, by the way, routinely forgot Syd's name and simply referred to him as "that guy with the pipe." I knew Jackie, and was aware of the enormous pressures on him during his live performances. When the show was over, he would relieve the tension by retreating to his dressing-room and weeping for hours at a time.

The better part of my early Hollywood experience was the social life. I knew some of the major figures at Warner Bros., including Charlie Einfeld, who was VP in charge of publicity; he had been a golfing buddy of mine in New York. I met Harry Warner's daughter, Doris, who was then married to Mervyn LeRoy and eventually became Billy Rose's fourth wife. I'd met Doris as a youngster in Mount Vernon. I eventually met many of the junior executives at Warners, Columbia Pictures, and MGM. Through these contacts I was an automatic invitee at poolside buffets. It was a great boon for a hostess to have one or two young, relatively personable men with clean fingernails and a smooth tongue. That was a pearl of great price at that time. A young single man could survive on literally nothing.

By that time, Ray Albert, a friend from New York, was my

roommate. He was a good-looking ex-insurance adjuster who had aspirations to movie stardom. After a weekend pool party, it was not unusual to get a phone call inviting us to a dinner party on the following Wednesday night. We became active on the "extra man" circuit, and could have had fourteen dinners a week. In Hollywood, if the inmates are not happy, they think they can send out for happiness, as if for Domino's Pizza.

Probably the best commission I ever got from Warners and Metro was to squire the budding starlets around Beverly Hills when they first arrived in California on their quest for fame. A young hopeful would arrive on the Twentieth Century Limited and I would meet her at the station, check her into a fancy hotel, buy her what she wanted at the best couturiers, escort her to dinner, and put it all on the studio's tab. Most of these moon-eyed girls never amounted to anything in the movies, but at least they never got into the wrong company while I kept the riff-raff away from them.

A couple of years later, when I was back in New York, Charlie Einfeld contacted me again and asked me to fulfill a similar function for the female cast members of George White's *Scandals*. The show had been touring and when it arrived in New York I took the young ladies to the City Athletic Club; there I tried to set them up with various friends, including Sylvan Coleman. On one occasion I was to escort Audrey Young, who later married Billy Wilder, but she was unable to make the date. Her roommate, Marie McDonald, accompanied me instead, and before she left for California I arranged singing lessons for her with a top vocal coach. Marie went on to some success in the movies, but she was tragically dead of an overdose by the age of forty-two.

The studios were caught in the Depression and were not anxious to hire any new talent, however promising. Syd and I wrote on speculation, barely surviving, but I felt uneasy, and the omens were grisly. I became impatient with the way everyone talked endlessly about whether they were going to get called, or if they were putting together a deal, or whether someone was worth talking to, or working for. It was a self-contained society that absolutely rejected any outside influences. The only thing that mattered was the movies.

The cultural lag was horrendous. During the first exhibit of Renoir's paintings in Hollywood one elderly lady and I were the only two visitors at the gallery between 11:00 A.M. and 3:00 P.M. Casual acquaintances addressed each other as "darling"; there was a phony effervescence, and a frenetic need to be seen. Oscar Levant was to remark one day, "Strip away the tinsel of Hollywood and you'll find the real tinsel underneath." Discussions of good books or world events were confined to a small intellectual elite which shunned the movie people and drew a subtle line between themselves as people of the theater and those who could remember only one line at a time. The exceptions were the British exiles, but they were so clannish that they were inaccessible and there was tremendous jealousy between them and the American actors who saw roles being stolen from them by the classically-trained Brits. There were (and are) some art aficionados in the industry: Kirk Douglas has a small, tasteful collection, and the finest personal gallery belonged to Edward G. Robinson. Edward was a remarkably different man in person than his usual screen persona of the tough guy. A speaker of several languages and an accomplished violinist, he was truly a Renaissance man, but he was also an anomaly in Hollywood.

The Brits were not the only little clan of emigrés to have an impact in Hollywood; there was also a wave of Magyars. Actors, singers, and beautiful starlets from Hungary were being wooed out to California by Harry Cohn. I had a friend named Fritz Tofanyi who was a producer in 1938 at MGM. Fritz was a very smart guy who knew that the novelty of writers having names like Roczi or Lazlo or Fiodor would only last so long. On the wall behind his desk hung a sampler which read: "It is not enough to be a Hungarian; you must also have a second act."

The studio system has been much maligned, but the fact is, the major movie companies provided a valuable education for young actors: they were able to learn diction, dancing, and deportment while being given the chance to perform in small screen roles for their studio.

There was also the lend-lease approach: if a distributor wanted to use a particular star, they would pay the player's studio for the privilege, though they often had to take whatever property was offered. The studios usually owned their own chains of cinemas, so even if a film was not particularly successful, at least the studio recouped some of its outlay on a production. Thanks to the government's dismantling of the vertically-integrated system, many of today's producers do not have that safety net.

Upon meeting someone, there was the inevitable question, "What do you do?" I would casually answer, "I am a writer," but you had to be careful to whom you spoke. I attended a dinner one evening with Hal, a writer friend of mine, who had a 1936 screenplay for Joan Bennett to his credit. Louis B. Mayer was in attendance and asked him what he had written. When Hal recounted with some pride his script for Miss Bennett, Mayer rebuked him, "That was two years ago. What have you written recently?" Hal lamely retorted, "I'm working on an idea now." Mayer turned away in disgust, saying, "You're not a writer."

Mayer himself was not infallible. When Mervyn LeRoy was directing *The Wizard of Oz*, Mayer wanted to cut out a song he thought was too childish and old-fashioned. LeRoy threatened to quit if the song did not remain in the picture, and that's why "Somewhere over the Rainbow" became one the greatest motion picture songs of all time.

Writing was a hazardous occupation for many reasons, as one of my relatives discovered to his cost. Harry Delf was not only my favorite cousin; he was a quadruple threat in the theater. In the Roaring Twenties he was a dancer, a singer, a composer and an author. One of his plays, *The Family Upstairs*, was a stage hit in 1927 and was made into a short film the following year, one of the first talking pictures ever. The characters in it were actually based on my own family!

Harry's performing career came to an abrupt end when an injury forced him to leave the stage in 1928, but he was the beneficiary of a remarkable insurance policy which paid him a substantial weekly amount. With this security to comfort him, Delf turned his attention to writing full-time. He poured out script after script and in the late thirties engaged the services of an RKO screen hack by the name of Harry Segall to assist him. Segall had a half-dozen films to his credit, but it was a play of Delf's which fired Segall's imagination. The story, about a reincarnated prizefighter, was called *Heaven Can Wait* (though it has also been known as *It Was Like This* and *Halfway to Heaven*). Segall took the idea to Everett Ruskin at Columbia Pictures, and the movie version emerged as *Here Comes Mr. Jordan*.

In 1941, Harry Delf sat in the mezzanine of Radio City Music Hall and watched his screenplay, with someone else's name on it, win an Oscar for Best Original Story. Segall not only made a lot of money for the picture, but went on to recycle the story in 1946 as *Angel On My Shoulder*, this time replacing God with the Devil, and a prizefighter with a gangster. Ironically, both films starred Claude Rains. Not surprisingly, the unaccredited and unpaid Harry Delf wanted no further truck with Harry Segall. Such are the vagaries of a writer's life.

Some years later I went to see Harry in an effort to persuade him to take a crack at Hollywood. I offered to put him in contact with my leads, but his spirit was broken and he preferred to stay at home and collect his weekly insurance check. He had established his own form of welfare dependency and wouldn't be budged out of his shelter.

In 1938, I gravitated to the company of novelists, gag writers, and the literati. I struck up a friendship with Marshall Grant, story editor of Universal Pictures, who liked our work, even if the studio heads did not.

I gradually came to know some of the popular writers in the movie colony: Sam and Bella Speewak, who wrote *Boy Meets Girl* and *Kiss Me, Kate*; Robert Riskin, who won an Oscar for his script for *It Happened One Night*; and Frances Marion, who had received Academy Awards for *The Big House* and *The Champ*.

There was a small building on the Metro lot called the short story building, where many would congregate. The short story department was under the control of Harry Rapf, a man possessed of an unusually large hooked nose. Rapf was much disliked on the Metro lot, perhaps as much for his "discovery" of the bitchy Joan Crawford as anything else. The writers liked to play a dice game called Roach, and the joke went that there was no danger of being caught by Rapf because his nose always gave ten minutes' warning of the arrival of rest of his body in the room. One of the staff writers, Dick Goldstein, once pitched Rapf a story about goblins: "See, they have these sharp pointy noses..." Rapf immediately nixed the story.

I overheard somebody complaining to Harry, "Why do you have to be so mean-spirited, talking down to them like that?" Harry said, "What do you mean? I love people." The other guy said, "Look at what you did to So-and-so," and he mentioned a particular star. Harry snorted, "What, an actor?"

Among Darryl Zanuck's stable of screenwriters was the eminently talented Nunnally Johnson, a man who had fitted very comfortably into the environment at the Algonquin. Born in Columbus, Georgia, just before the turn of the century, he began his writing career in journalism. He worked on local newspapers until he moved to New York in 1918 to take up a position at the *Herald-Tribune*. He eventually started to write short stories, some of which were published in the *Saturday Evening Post* and later collected into a 1930 book entitled *There Ought to Be a Law*.

One of the *Post* stories was called "Rough House Rosie," and in 1927 it became the basis for a film starring the "It" girl, Clara Bow. Inspired by this success, Nunnally moved to Hollywood in 1932 and became one of Darryl Zanuck's busiest writers at Twentieth Century-Fox. His motion picture career reached its apogee in 1940 with his adaptation of Steinbeck's *The Grapes of Wrath*, which was heralded as a monumental achievement for the cinema and nominated for an Academy Award.

When I met Johnson in 1938, we discovered we had a common interest in startling or amusing names. My maiden aunt Louise was a public school teacher, and through the portals of her classroom passed students bearing enchanting names, such as Apple Blossom Epstein, that positively begged for repetition. The family spent a wonderful evening creating a fiction around young Miss Epstein, and, encouraged by this, Aunt Louise reported each promising new arrival in her class. Clarence De Courtney Rosenberg appeared a winner for some time, but then came Ike Meltz and Jake Schmelts. My aunt could not miss that opportunity and started calling them as a dual entry. She would posit a question and then call out, "Schmelts and Meltz!" and then accept their joint answers as one.

While I was in Hollywood there was an Austrian-born actress who had starred in *Abie's Irish Rose* in Vienna. She bore the unlikely name of Gisela Werbezink-Piffl, which no one believed when introduced to her. She appeared in a screenplay written by Nunnally, and long after the picture was finished, he kept thinking about the lady. She so occupied his mind that one day at the Friar's Club, somewhat emboldened by a few libations, he looked her up in the Los Angeles telephone book. Finding the number, he called and asked to speak to Madam Gisela Werbezink-Piffl. "This is Madam Piffl" was the response. Nunnally continued that this was Charlie from Kansas City calling. Werbezink-Piffl, suspicious, said, "I have never been in Kansas City and I don't know any Charlie." With feigned surprise, Johnson said, "I can't believe that you have forgotten so soon." With a note of finality, Gisela said, "I told you, I have never been in Kansas City." Johnson reluctantly said: "Then I guess it must have been another Gisela Werbezink-Piffl."

On another occasion, Nunnally told me of an obituary

which he had clipped out of a London newspaper. It noted the passing of Colonel Reginald Bastard, who had in any event lived to be almost eighty years of age and probably endured some rather heavy-handed ribaldry during his life. Johnson used to write letters to Frank Sullivan in Saratoga and receive letters in return, in which they would exult in new discoveries. I do not recall who dug up Mrs. Birdie Bottom Tingle, but it was a winner. The favorite appeared in the wedding banns published in *The New York Times*. They heralded the nuptials of Miss Alice Foxhall, who proposed to marry a gent by the name of Knight, apparently without thinking of the terrible consequences of a hyphenated name.

✧ ✧ ✧

I was invited to dinners and events which were attended by Bob Benchley, Alan Campbell, and Dorothy Parker. Dottie had been chewed up by the movie system, but she spat it right back with her trenchant work on such films as *A Star is Born*. The fact that she was making regular money for the first time in her life probably helped divert the slings and arrows of outrageous Hollywood. Money was the principal justification for the Round Tablers to stay in Hollywood. They hated the weather and the vacuous attitude, preferring loud confrontations in dark, smoke-filled rooms with the paint peeling from the walls.

I renewed my friendship with Abe Burrows, City College graduate and a Wall Street colleague, who had moved west at about the same time I had. Abe was an entertaining fellow at parties, where he would sing his offbeat ditties, like "The Girl With the Three Blue Eyes," at the piano. One of the funniest anecdotes Abe recounted to me was from his childhood, when it was fashionable for women to wear flowers in their elaborate hats. When the Burrows family was finally able to move from the city to the suburbs, Abe was thrilled to discover that they now had a garden. In his excitement, he turned to his father and piped, "Pop! We could grow something! How do you grow flowers?" Came the laconic reply, "What am I? A milliner?"

Abe ultimately found fame and fortune with the film of *Guys and Dolls*, for which he co-wrote the book, but he started out in Hollywood writing jokes for a show called "Duffy's Tavern," starring Ed Gardner. Abe told me that the first joke he sold was to Gardner's agent, Swifty Lazar, for two dollars. Swifty was a small, bald, roly-poly man, with huge black horn rim glasses; he looked for all the world like a rich child's beach ball from F. A. O. Schwartz. Lazar went on to become the most successful literary agent in America well into the late 1970s, representing major world figures such as Henry Kissinger. That was a pretty far cry from a two dollar joke.

I began to squire Anita Louise, a beautiful young lady who was a star of the second magnitude at Warner Bros. She was intelligent, unpretentious, and grand company. She was then playing in *Green Light* opposite Errol Flynn, with whom we often lunched at the studio. Flynn was a wild character whose cronies included John Decker, Fred McEvoy, Bruce Cabot, and W. C. Fields. To fool around with them when they were in their cups (which was almost always) was to take your life in your hands. I had met Fields at a party and found him to be every bit the curmudgeon he was reputed to be. Flynn had a house at Mulholland Ranch which had two-way mirrors in strategic places. The floor and ceiling show was notorious!

Errol Flynn was as handsome in real life as he was on screen. Unfortunately, the high life he lived eventually left him flabby and puffy. Michael Curtiz, who directed Flynn in 1935's *Captain Blood*, could entertain us for an entire evening with his stories of how he had to shoot the Australian star from dozens of different angles in order to get as much of Errol as possible into the picture. Curtiz did not, however, have a high opinion of his leading man's acting ability, and found the swashbuckler very irresponsible and pugnacious. The studio would have loved to unload him, but the public adored him and would never have allowed it.

Anita and I were witness to some of the excesses of the big studio brass. For example, Darryl Zanuck was the major pooh-bah at Twentieth Century-Fox. His favorite sport was polo and with a wave of Fox's magic checkbook he hired Aidan Roark and Cecil Smith, two international polo-playing buddies, for the sum of a thousand dollars a week each. He also engaged the services of Fidel La Barba, a professional boxer, to help keep himself in shape. The shareholders were being skewered.

On occasion, Anita and I visited the posh Clover Club on Sunset Strip, which housed games of chance. It would shut down for three or four months every year while the community regained its financial equilibrium. Money was a stranger to me, and Anita was not the gambling type, so we would only risk ten dollars between us. Remember, I had left the bulk of my Wall Street earnings with my family in New York. After paying the rent of forty dollars a month on my Hollywood apartment, I budgeted a mere sixteen dollars a week for my other expenditures. Not exactly the lap of luxury!

At the Clover, caviar and champagne were free, so it was a great deal. Anita's presence at the blackjack tables brought players flocking, and the dealer arranged matters so that she never won enough to quit, but never lost it all. Once, in order to beat a high roller, the dealer had to beat Anita, who had bet ten dollars. As soon as the house won, he quickly threw twenty dollars in front of her. He didn't want to lose a good shill.

I discussed this with Nick the Greek, the famous professional gambler of the time, who had the reputation of being very straight. (We assumed that because he was still in full possession of his limbs.) After listening to my tale, he opined that there wasn't a straight gambling house in the United States; they cheated because that was their nature.

Later that evening, I watched as Zanuck dropped a massive amount of money at roulette. He shed no tears for this mishap, and we soon found out why. A few weeks later, an item in the Hollywood Reporter noted that the proprietor of the Clover Club, a member of Detroit's infamous Purple Gang, had been hired on a forty-week contract at a thousand a week by Twentieth Century-Fox to supervise the various gambling scenes in the pictures. Zanuck had just happened to lose exactly forty thousand dollars.

Twentieth Century-Fox was essentially controlled by Chase National Bank, although there were other banks in the syndicate. William Fox, the owner of Fox Studios, was a distant cousin of my mother. During the Depression, he pledged his studio's stock against a loan from Chase National Bank. After the Crash, Winthrop Aldrich Rockefeller was appointed head of the bank, and when Fox could not meet the deadline for his loan repayment, Chase immediately seized the studio as fulfillment of the debt. I was sitting at the desk of a silk-stocking trader called Pynchom and Company when I heard the news. It all took place in a matter of hours, just as later banks would take over H. L. Green Stores and Lehman Brothers. That is just one of the reasons I have never used only one bank in my life.

In 1935, after the merger between Fox Studios and Twentieth Century, Chase found itself to be the proud possessor of a money-making machine.

William Fox did not fare so well. In 1934, he was convicted of stock market manipulation by a Senate investigation committee and jailed for a year. After his release, he discovered that his many showbiz "friends" were no longer taking his calls. In the same investigation, it was revealed that Chase had recklessly gambled $70 million of depositors' money on Fox stocks. The investigation was the first shot fired in the government's war on the vertical integration of the studio system.

When I returned to New York at the end of 1938, I could scarcely wait to call my friend, John Dillon, chairman of the finance committee at Chase, and regale him with tales of management excesses at Twentieth Century. John patiently explained to me that Chase had intimate knowledge of this and of other phenomena that would surprise even me. Determined to put an end to this financial rape, Chase had instituted a practice of sending eager young executives to California to go over the books with the accountants. They had even resorted to sending uncorrupted new graduates from the Harvard Business School. The story was always the same.

A studio representative would meet the potential inquisitor on the Super Chief at Chicago. He would have with him a beautiful young lady, and enough liquor to last until the arrival in California. A limousine would then drive the banker to a cottage at the Beverly Hills Hotel, where there was much festivity, but little discussion of work. These forays might last as long as two or three weeks, and the recovery period for the representative would last about the same time. The constant repetition made the bank throw their hands up and they ceased this practice. So much for my crusade for a cleaner and better Hollywood.

About one year later, Dillon summoned me to explain that Chase had a very shaky loan to a company called Educational Grand National Pictures, presided over by a man who had a wonderful mind until it was made up. Dillon reminded me of my desire to clean up the mess in Hollywood and he put me in charge of the reorganization of Educational Grand National.

I confidently made my appearance the next morning at their plush offices in Rockefeller Center and discovered that the organization had mastered the art of repose. They religiously followed three rigid rules:

1. Don't stand if you can sit down.

2. Don't sit if you can lie down.

3. Never confuse anybody with the facts.

I spent four incredible months interviewing incompetents and liars, and I never caught one of them in the truth. Humbled, I called my friends at the bank and suggested that they turn the key in the lock and sell the furniture.

In my peregrinations in Hollywood, I had gotten to know George Hearst, the profligate son of William Randolph Hearst. To a lesser degree, I also knew George's brothers Jack and Randy Hearst, and this qualified me for an invitation to San Simeon. Hearst Newspapers had Louella Parsons on their staff; she was the most powerful columnist in motion pictures, and everyone danced to her tune. Because of her influence, the Hearst boys were lionized by the Hollywood crowd.

William Randolph Hearst was cut from a rough bolt of cloth. His relationship with Marion Davies was as well known as the melody of "Jingle Bells," though he simply refused to discuss it. "I am not saying it's right. I'm saying it is," he declared flatly. On an impulse, Hearst had bought St. Donat's Castle in

Glamorgan, Wales, but never used it as a home. When his wife was told it was Norman, she reportedly asked, "Norman who?" It was sometime later that Hearst bought San Simeon.

San Simeon is a massive, gleaming white structure which Mr. Hearst had disassembled stone by stone and reconstructed on a hilltop on the coast of California, a place so remote that it seemed to me that only the Artful Dodger would ever find it. It was, of course, the model for Xanadu in Orson Welles's *Citizen Kane*.

A startling and overpowering impression was created at the guests' first sight of the great dining hall. A gothic fireplace of incredible size dominated the space. Hanging high above the refectory table, which seated forty or fifty people, were medieval banners from Siena in Northern Italy. These pennants were used during the Palio, reputedly the most dangerous horse race in the world, where young Italians risk their lives riding wild-eyed stallions over the uneven Sienese cobblestones. (The festival is so named after the Italian word for straw, which is scattered on the ground to afford traction for the horses' hooves.) The flags were now at rest in the Hearst dining room, but they readily conjured visions of medieval times.

The most important people in the world might, at one time or another, have been guests. The châtelaine was Marion Davies. Miss Davies was a very attractive girl of limited acting ability, but Hearst was determined that she would appear in pictures, so he founded Cosmopolitan Pictures and arranged a distribution agreement with MGM for the sole purpose of making her a star. Her notices were never sensational, but in the Hearst newspapers at least, she received rave reviews. Anyone who unduly criticized her would incur the wrath of the vituperative Louella Parsons.

Marion Davies, youngest daughter of a New York City magistrate by the name of Douras (a position bought by Mr.

Hearst), did not make any waves as a movie star, but as a drinker she was nationally ranked. She indulged in this sport at every opportunity and became extremely proficient. Hearst had seen the results of overindulgence and published a ban on alcohol at San Simeon. This scarcely caused Marion any distress as she stashed liquor away in toilet tanks, bushes, and guest closets.

Another forbidden exercise in the sacrosanct precinct of San Simeon was the enjoyment of sexual relations with anyone other than your spouse. Given the fact that Davies and the still-married Hearst were man and mistress, this prohibition of the sampling of forbidden fruit would seem strange; it was, nonetheless, a hard and fast rule.

Dorothy Parker ran afoul of both of Hearst's dicta. One unfortunate night, in 1936, she was caught *in flagrante delicto* by one of the Hearst retainers. Directed to leave at the crack of dawn, before the firing squad could form, Dorothy was groggily stumbling out when she noticed the Visitors' Book. She immediately dropped bag and baggage and entered the following rhyme for posterity:

"Upon my honor
I saw a Madonna
Standing in a niche
Above the door
Of the famous whore
Of a prominent son of a bitch."

Syd Zelinka and I were shepherded from studio to studio by Al Leeds of the Landau Leeds Agency. They handled stars of the magnitude of Jean Harlow and William Powell; now here they were trying to peddle our latest fascinating tale.

Al Leeds in New York and Arthur Landau wanted a younger man to come in and manage their business. Charlie Einfeld recommended me to their agency for the job, and Leeds was very keen for me to handle the finances of his biggest clients; for one split second I thought, "Why not?" Then I realized I would have to deal with actors, so I declined the offer. Would could have predicted the enormous power and influence that business managers and agents like Michael Ovitz would eventually wield in Hollywood? I clearly recall, however, Charlie Einfeld's words of warning to me: "I'll back you in anything you want, except the movie picture business. You want to open a restaurant that serves the greatest pizza in the world, get a recipe; I'll back you."

Through Al I met Jerry Wald, a writer and, later, a producer at Warner Bros. Jerry was reported to be the basis for the character of Sammy Glick in Budd Schulberg's book *What Makes Sammy Run*, and he certainly had the energy to match his fictional counterpart. Jerry started out in the late 1920s as a copy boy on the *Graphic* in New York. He came from a painfully poor family and always had to wear his older brother's cast-off shoes, which never fit him properly. When Jerry got successful, he filled his closets with hundreds of pairs of shoes.

Wald was not a great writer, but when it came to telling and selling a story, he was a real hustler. One afternoon, Jerry and I were driving to the Rose Bowl with Junior Laemmle, former head of Universal Pictures. Without using actual names, Jerry related the story of how sportscaster Ted Husing was barred from Harvard University football games for a remark he had made over the airwaves. Apparently, the Crimson's quarterback had got his signals crossed and the play broke down. In disgust, Husing blurted out, "God! What a putrid play!" After his disbarment, Ted would surreptitiously sneak a microphone into the stadium under cover of a huge chrysanthemum and call the game in secrecy from the stands. As Jerry warmed to his tale, Junior, whose fortunes had been thin of late, demanded to know if the story was for sale. Jerry smelled green and said, "Sure it is." Junior promptly bought this "original" Wald story for a cool fifty grand.

One night, Ray Albert and I cooked dinner at home and we had Jerry over. When the meal was over, we sat around smoking and shooting the breeze; Jerry said, "I've just come up with this incredible story. Would you like to hear it?" We then sat mesmerized for thirty minutes while he told us this fabulous story, lavish with details and peopled with vivid characters. When it was over, he got up and said, "I've got to be at the studio tomorrow." Ray and I just sat there in stunned silence. That son of a bitch had just told us Conrad's *Heart of Darkness*.

As the summer of 1938 waned, I began to take a more realistic view of Hollywood. There were certainly small jobs for acolytes who administered to the slightest whim of illiterate executives, but I didn't see a future in that. Being constantly in the company of empty-headed narcissists soon loses its charm. I could forgive Hollywood for being the refuge of phonies; I could never forgive it for being a bore. "They say that California adds ten years to your life," said Harry Ruby, perfectly capturing my sentiments, "Well, I'd like to spend those ten years in New York."

One day, I returned to my apartment, packed my bags, paid up my rent, and started the long drive back East.

Charles, New York, circa 1938

6

BACK ON SQUARE ONE

There is a famous scene at the end of Balzac's *Pere Goriot* right after the funeral of the title character: Eugene Rastignac, the young protagonist, standing in Pere Lachaise cemetery and gazing down at the vast nocturnal panorama of the Paris he has as yet been unable to conquer, hurls out a challenge to the city, "*A nous deux maintenant*"; roughly translated, this means, "Let's go — just the two of us — I'm ready for you now." I understand how he felt. I looked at New York with the same eyes in 1938, although I can't place this feeling in a specifically dramatic or novelistic moment (staring out from the recently completed Rockefeller Center, for example, at the New York skyline). In the eyes of my family and the world, I was twenty-eight years old, broke, back on square one: other than a tan, I had nothing to show for my brief period of indenture in the movie colony. Nevertheless, I knew I was ready to make a move.

Strategically retreating to my old haunts in Wall Street, I temporarily hung my hat in the office of Allen & Co., where I kept myself out of the soup kitchen by bringing in a few small deals on commission. Allen & Co. was not yet the top-ranking international deal maker it later became (engineering the famous Columbia pictures deal with Coca-Cola and Sony, for example, or acting as bankers for Rupert Murdoch) but it was in the process of becoming a force on the Street. Charlie Allen, an old friend of mine, had only a minimal formal education and did not do business in a traditional way, but rarely has one man had such an ability to cut through the haze and determine the underlying value of a proposed deal. He had a very short attention span, however, so one of my functions was to listen to a customer's pitch, and elicit the salient facts, a process which could take two hours or more. I would then outline the proposal for Charlie in about five minutes and make my recommendations.

One day, a defrocked rabbi by the name of Cohen proposed a deal to Charlie which appeared to be foolproof, but something about this gentleman worried me. I informed Charlie that he would not lose money if he protected himself, but my nose told me that our ex-rabbi was a crook and I recommended that Charlie pass. Charlie Allen was not a volatile character, but he angrily delivered an impassioned philippic:

"You are right, he is a crook, but I would rather do business with a crook than a friend, because I will watch a crook closely, while I will not watch a friend. It may surprise you to know that a friend will disappoint and screw you."

With that, Charlie said we would do the deal. I denounced him as a fool, but sixty days later, Mr. Cohen, although he was thrashing about like a school of sharks, delivered as he had promised, a profitable and successful deal for Allen & Co. Charles Allen was one of the wealthiest and most successful men of our time.

As I listened to people petitioning Allen & Co. with ideas

and dreams, I began to frame in my mind the appropriate solution to my own future. The air was filled with rumors of new types of aircraft being developed in remote laboratories. By today's standards it was pretty low-tech, but at the time it sounded as if impossible scientific barriers were being shattered. I had read Billy Mitchell's book on air power, and I was convinced that, as things were going in Europe, the need for air supremacy was not to be taken lightly. One morning, I sat in the subway on the way to work and read the following headline: "'I HATE WAR': FDR." The essence of the accompanying story was that President Roosevelt would never send American boys to die on foreign battlefields. I had a good track record in translating FDR and I knew just what to do.

A friend named Jack Milliken knew an engineer whom he claimed was the French equivalent of Steinmetz, the German scientist who played a major role at General Electric. As Jack and I both agreed that aircraft was going to play a vital role in the coming war, we set out to find a small aircraft parts manufacturing company that was in financial straits. We found a machine shop which was within the means of our limited capital in a loft on Grand Street in lower New York. We called our grand enterprise Atlas Aircraft Products Corporation.

Our French wizard set about organizing machinery and hiring a small staff, while Jack and I presented ourselves to Grumman Aircraft, Republic Aviation, and Brewster Aircraft as expert subcontractors for small parts. We were well received, and enlisted an adjacent machine shop to help us manage our affairs for a share of any profits. Within six months, Atlas Aircraft took off into clear skies, but there was a dark cloud on the horizon. Our French engineer was an impostor who knew no more than an ordinary machinist. While we were busy looking for business, he demonstrated a talent for making worthless scrap out of very expensive steel, which was already in short supply.

The discovery of a huge pile of unmarked steel scrap revealed the awful truth. Unless the situation were immediately corrected, we were on our way to trouble, so we ditched our Gallic interloper and set about finding some real, honest-to-goodness technical talent.

Events in Europe were now reaching a critical point. There was still a tremendous isolationist feeling in the United States, and Roosevelt managed to get the Selective Service Law passed by only one vote in Congress. The significant and statesmanlike intervention of Republican Senator Vandenberg of Michigan decided the issue. He was convinced that FDR was right, and his heroic bi-partisan effort brought many Republicans to an understanding of the dangers facing us all.

Large American corporations now held seminars to display blueprints of parts they needed to fill orders which were pouring in from England, France, Australia, and Canada. General Motors sponsored such a show at Grand Central Palace in New York City. There I met a very attractive young man by the name of Robert Cox, who impressed me so much that within fifteen minutes I had hired him as the new chief engineer for Atlas Aircraft Products Corp.

Bob immediately reorganized the production lines, recommended the purchase of new equipment, and re-evaluated our existing contracts. "Scrap" disappeared instantly from our vocabulary.

I was not about to be trapped again with any second-rate engineers who were being fobbed off as the likes of Steinmetz, so I enrolled in New York University night school to study electrical engineering so that I might, at least, be able to have intelligent discussions with Bob. We came to the inevitable conclusion that we needed a strong engineering team, but since engineers were in great demand, this was a formidable challenge.

Some of the best technical talent in Europe was fleeing Germany, so I pursued several avenues toward making contact with these refugees and found a brilliant design engineer. Simon Saretzky was Russian-born but German-educated. He was working for the Boston firm of Halsey Cabot where, because he was Jewish and spoke with a very strong accent, he had few friends. Through him I was also successful in acquiring a Czech engineer by the name of Jan Wohryzek. Jan, a production engineer of extraordinary talent and a graduate of the Technical Institute in Vienna, completed our engineering triumvirate. As long as we could guarantee our immigrant workers a job, and vouch for their reliability, they were legally permitted to stay in the country.

Our main customer was the United States government. A brand new entity, the Smaller War Plans Corporation, which loaned federal money to small businesses, came into being. Almost no one knew of its existence. I went to them with the hope of borrowing a hundred thousand dollars, but as I talked to the gentleman who ran the office I realized there was much more to be had. I wasn't exactly sure what I would do with the loan, but the terms were so generous that I finally took out a capital loan of one million dollars. Our company was the very first to receive a loan of this kind.

We now had the necessary funds to start operating. We had engineering, we had planning; all we needed was marketing. I had spent some time in Washington, D.C., and through my personal contacts with the military we were able to develop valuable business leads, to say nothing of a good reputation for efficiency and honesty.

At Atlas Aircraft (as we named our company) we never stopped looking for better engineers or better marketing people. A friend of my brother Bill was our extremely efficient expediter; when we ordered material we'd usually have it within eight days. We were given certain allocations of steel by the War Production Board for any specific contract. We would present the contract number to the Board, they would assign a priority, and the steel company would deliver accordingly. I knew most of the aluminum and steel suppliers and, because we understood what made things move, we built a great little company.

We first had to bid on a contract, and when it was completed the Renegotiation Board would examine our books and check up on our qualifications. If they thought we'd made too much money on the contract, they'd take back, say, three hundred thousand dollars. This was perfectly fair because there were unscrupulous people who were buying and selling worthless goods just to make more money. We made a point of delivering top quality equipment because, in the last analysis, somebody has to pay for the excesses performed by the government or by people who sell to the government. In the war effort, the lives of a lot of people and the safety of the country depended on our ability to make high quality at a reasonable price. It was simply the right thing to do.

Back in 1927 (in Erie, Pennsylvania to be precise) I took a chance for fifty cents and won an airplane and eight hours of instruction in a raffle. When I had completed my training I flew back to New York by following the Pennsylvania railroad tracks; when I saw the 59th Street Bridge, I flew out to Long Island and landed on Roosevelt Field. I kept the plane until 1937, using it for many business and social ventures. And now here I was making airplane parts. It was the last thing I thought I'd ever be doing and, in a totally unexpected way, it had an important effect on my life.

In the course of my peregrinations about town with Jack Milliken, I met John Jacob Astor Junior who took an interest in our business. He made a practice of coming to the office at about ten o'clock in the morning, and seating himself next to my desk until about four, counting that, I suppose, as a work day. He was never introduced to anybody in the labor force, and never took part in any of the business discussions. He was a figure of great mystery, and the staff dubbed him Secret Sam.

Astor saw himself as a Romeo and became infatuated with a beautiful, amusing, and mischievous show girl by the name of Vera Shea. I introduced Vera to Secret Sam and they became a duo who divided their time between the La Martinique nightclub and Cartier's. Vera, who had been Marie McDonald's roommate, later returned the favor by playing Cupid for me. After Marie had gone to star in Hollywood musicals, Vera called me up and said, "I have a friend who is even nicer than Marie; let me introduce you." And that was how I met my wife, Rose.

She was a great beauty, much loved by her peers in the musical theater. Despite these credentials, it was necessary to rescue her from a musical horror christened *Allah Be Praised*, which was still in rehearsal. The cast was at the Shubert Theater in Philadelphia, having roundly defeated three writers' attempts to improve the script. If the show had opened in that condition in New York, there might have been bloodshed on the stage. The producer, Alfred Bloomingdale, a scion of the department store family, in desperation sent to California for Cy Howard, successful comedy writer, a tweedy type with leather patches at the elbows. Cy witnessed a run-through in silence and made no comment. After a long pause, during which he bit his nails, Bloomingdale fearfully asked for the verdict. Howard turned to him and recommended that he "close the

Rose, bread company commercial studio shot *circa* 1940

show and keep the store open nights." Released from indenture to Bloomingdale, Rose was "at liberty."

After a brief career as a model in her native Chicago, where she was variously the Coca Cola Girl and the Chesterfield Girl, Rose won a beauty contest which included a screen test at Warner Bros. Warners did not know a good thing when they saw one and missed a star. Rose, unfazed, headed for New York to seek her fame and fortune, leaving the talent scouts in shock.

Sophie Tucker was a major star in the thirties and forties, attracting mainly the Broadway crowd. She was billed as The Last of the Red Hot Mommas, and played the Palace and the Keith vaudeville circuit in addition to nightclubs. She teamed with George Jessel in a forgettable revue called *High Kickers*, which opened (auspiciously enough) on Halloween, 1941, at the Broadhurst Theater. It ran for one hundred and seventy-one performances, and featured Rose Teed with her good friend Joyce Matthews as "Two American Showgirls." Joyce, an eye-popping blonde, added a touch of spice to the headlines by marrying Milton Berle exactly twice. This kind of publicity never hurt a show, and is manna from heaven for the press agent. To demonstrate that she played no favorites, Joyce later committed matrimony with Billy Rose an equal number of times. In each case, there was one time of interruption, occasioned by a divorce.

The chorus line was beautiful, and Tommy Manville, the asbestos heir playboy, married two of the ladies in the ensemble and proposed to two more, including my wife. One of his marriages was to Bonnie Edwards, who was a stunning girl. Years later, Rose was to remark, "My most stable friend has been married six times." She was on the mark. Bonnie's marital extravaganza created the name Bonita Edwards Manville Barbie Babst Wilson Biegel Silberstein. Ben Silberstein was the unhappy father-in-law of Ivan Boesky and had disliked him from the beginning. Ben's daughter, Seema, must be lamenting that she did not listen to dear old Dad.

During *High Kickers*, Rose and Joyce squealed their electrifying lines in unison to a mesmerized audience: "Here come those two American millionaires now!" They were instantly enshrined with Helen Hayes and Lynn Fontanne. Our nuptials followed shortly after the demise of *Allah Be Praised*, in 1944. I was thirty-four and Rose was twelve years my junior. The only sadness attendant on the occasion of our union was that my mother had recently died.

Jack Milliken did not find himself addicted to the business, and I bought him out. He was commissioned a lieutenant in the U.S. Navy, attached to the bureau of personnel. We remained lifelong friends, but in business terms, I was once again on my own.

The Atlas Aircraft team quickly developed a reputation for imagination and quality, and we soon grew out of not one, but two new plants. By the time the United States entered the war, we had grown into a very smooth and successful business manufacturing generators and delicate instrument motors. We changed our name to Cyclohm Motor Corporation and moved to a large factory in Long Island City. I never did thank the Nazis properly for making such great talent available.

I actually worked in the plant, though I had no technical background except that, as a kid, I built a crystal radio set. But I had a notion of what it was all about and as I watched some of the machinists handle the tool press I thought, "What is the big deal? I can do that." It also gave me a sense later on, when we

a fair
grum-
ld pay
s, and
They
their
d of a

e was
g the
Mil-
of St.
ellow
ow in

ed in
h, he
ahili.

gov
ld

generators that weighed thousands of
ermine how much something cost to
how to wind the armatures, about ma-
ɔ cold roll and hot roll.

ge organization to prepare the bids in
ys, but I discovered that if, instead of
ous process of estimating every nuance
weighed the material and then multi-
pecified, we could then safely make our
ive enough to ensure we won the con-

c to our formula; just simple common
discovered that since 1917, the Navy
thousand dollars apiece to a company
or a motor generator. I saw a procure-
I was visiting my brother Bill, who was
terial in St. Louis. I asked him for the
and when I looked at them it didn't take
t it would cost Cyclohm twenty-five hun-
ime generator. When we bid the contract,
lder by five grand.

have the Navy send me a model of the gener-
yzed everything, I saw that there was a certain
d steel that they had prescribed in the bidding
not used in the model they sent me. This steel
to machine; I smelled a rat right away. The Navy
e major bidders to make one generator to specifi-
ɔ cost us about fourteen thousand. Cyclohm made
t was exactly to specifications.

down to the admiral in charge and just laid the facts
for him. I said "Now, you can make me deliver on that
ɔ and I will. In the process, however, I will go bankrupt

and you will not get your product. Or you can pay me
price, since I am the only who met the specs." After some
bling and lecturing, we came up with a solution: they wou
a hundred thousand dollars for my model and my drawing
give the contract to the other bidders. Everybody won.
were able to go back to their sweetheart, *and* take care o
suitor. I couldn't have done that if I hadn't had some kin
feel for what was being done on the floor.

As the events in Europe dominated the headlines, the
a substantial rush to enlist or seek a commission. Amor
eager candidates for the latter was a mutual friend of Jack
liken and myself, whom we shall call Ferdie. A graduate
Paul's and Princeton, he was an exceedingly attractive
who was the sole surviving heir to a rather large fortune n
the hands of an aging aunt.

Ferdie thought his military talents could best be us
naval intelligence, and though he spoke flawless Frenc
made the outlandish claim on his résumé that he spoke Sv

Ferdie convinced his aunt that, instead of wearing the
ernment issue uniform of a lieutenant junior grade, it wou
more appropriate, given the family status, to have his uni
tailor-made. The night before he was to appear in Washi
to be commissioned, Ferdie admired his handsome new
form so much that he strolled to his usual oasis, El Mor
omitting to wear his uniform cap in the street, an offense
parable to barratry.

At El Morocco, Ferdie became embroiled in an alterc
with a male patron over the affections of a young woman

bar. The ensuing brouhaha unfortunately attracted the attention of a captain in the U.S. Navy, who immediately demanded of Ferdie his name and his billet. Ferdie replied that he lived at the Hotel Madison, and was going to Washington on the morrow to receive his commission. The Captain, incensed at this impersonation of an officer in the U.S. Navy, ordered Ferdie to return to his hotel and stay there until he was sent for.

The next morning, two hostile bluejackets escorted Ferdie to the Navy bureau of personnel in Washington. There followed a scene that was frighteningly reminiscent of the Dreyfus case in Paris, as an officer tore the buttons and the epaulettes from Ferdie's tailor-made uniform.

Ferdie's next privilege was to be inducted as a private in the U.S. Army and assigned to an Army camp near Washington, D.C. Ferdie was not to be deterred. He had the money to hire limousines and soon became a popular figure by arranging dates for colonels, majors, and even a few brigadier-generals, with the entire female population of Washington between the ages of eighteen and thirty. It was a lovely war.

Sad to relate, Ferdie came a cropper on the rocks of a romance with a very rich widow with connections. In a moment of carelessness, he borrowed $10,000 from her, and apparently forgot to repay it. The lady made a few telephone calls, and Ferdie was transferred to the Aleutian Islands where he spent the rest of the war trying to avoid freezing to death while ruminating on his delinquencies.

Our local draft board had three men by the name of Wohlstetter living within its jurisdiction. Albert, my younger brother, had obtained his Ph.D. at Columbia and accepted a

Rockefeller Fellowship in mathematics. When the war enveloped the United States, Arthur Burns, who was studying business cycles at the Rockefeller Foundation, summoned Albert to Washington to work on the Planning Committee of the War Production Board. Albert's statistical analysis skills were effectively channeled.

I was involved in the design and manufacture of essential hand-driven generators used by the Marines during their island-hopping in the Pacific theater, to provide instant electric power for the transmission of communication signals.

In 1941, I received the first of several communiqués requiring my presence at the draft board, but the Marine Corps would frustrate any efforts at inducting me by requesting that I be furloughed for the duration because of my importance to the war effort.

Actually going to the draft board was the most awful experience of your life. The board told you. "Take the subway over and keep the five cents fare. Don't bring any money." You literally never knew if you'd be going home or straight into the Army.

The board held their physicals at Grand Central Palace on Lexington and 43rd. You would got undressed down to the ignominy of your socks and shoes, and carry your pants, shirt, and coat on your arm. You would then be crammed uncomfortably close together on an interminable line until you were marched into a room to be examined by a doctor. He'd bark, "Read that chart." Then they'd shuffle you to the next medic, who examined your teeth, and so on down the line until finally, as a last insult, you saw a psychiatrist. Don't ask me why that one! Some of those guys in line, I can assure you, needed a bath more than they needed a shrink.

Three times I was summoned; three times the Marines intervened. By that time, I had had so much blood removed and been manhandled so vigorously by the Army's doctors that I believed I would be safer on a battlefield; but the Marines and the Signal Corps finally prevailed and I was furloughed.

That left only Bill, my older brother, age forty. The draft board seemed determined that somebody by the name of Wohlstetter was going to be in uniform, so I discussed with my brother the choice of either being drafted as the oldest man in the United States infantry, or becoming an officer and a gentleman in the United States Navy. I assured him that I had the means to virtually guarantee him a commission, and though he scoffed, he authorized me to get the necessary documents.

My friend Sylvan was then a deputy to James Forrestal, the Secretary of the Navy. He had contrived this happy position through the good offices of his friend Frank Folson, who was then head of RCA. At the outbreak of hostilities, Folson recommended Sylvan to a post at the Navy Office of Procurement, and from there his natural charm took him into Forrestal's protection. I now appealed to him for assistance, and I obtained all the essential papers, but several weeks wore on with no word from the Navy.

It was the Friday afternoon before Columbus Day, and Bill reached me in French Lick, Indiana, to tell me that he had to appear on the following Tuesday for a physical examination that would lead to his induction into the Army. What had happened to his commission? I called Sylvan to explain the urgency and he ran down the hall to Secretary Forrestal's office. There were four thousand commissions on his desk waiting to be signed but Sylvan extricated my brother's papers. Forrestal, who was going away for the long weekend, signed them with one hand on a pen and one hand in the sleeve of his overcoat. I got back to Bill and told him that he was being commissioned the following Monday. When he inquired how he should respond to his draft board, I said, "Tell them to salute you."

Before the war, Bill had a steady business as a commercial auctioneer, appraising machinery and machine tools. He would buy bankrupt factories and auction the contents; eventually he became president of the Auctioneers Association. Because of this background, he knew the performance values and characteristics of machine tools, and thus evolved into an expert. As such, Bill was a valuable asset to Navy procurement so when he was commissioned as a lieutenant senior grade, they assigned him to the inspector of naval materiel.

Cyclohm was a solid success, but as the war in Europe wound down, I began to consider the future of hand-crank generators in peace time. Our engineers began to look at the commercial use of products that had been developed during the war, such as the facsimile, which was devised as a means for aircraft to send back pictures of targets which they had identified. After the war, Western Union tried to adapt the fax to their commercial requirements, and they needed a small specialized rotating machine. Until then, they had either been making these motors by hand at ridiculous cost, or buying them from itinerant garage-type operations. As a result, every machine was different and therefore expensive.

Cyclohm examined their needs and designed an entire line of motors which could standardize and supply the various operating characteristics they required. So, with imagination and planning, we invented the special motor business.

In Charlie Allen's opinion, I was an accident of the war, and he advised me to sell my manufacturing business before my masquerade was revealed. But I also had an obligation to the people who had made our success possible. I created a leveraged buyout to include all department heads and the people who had figured in the building of the company. Inventory and machinery would be paid for over a long period of time at original cost. I retained the cash assets and the building for my portion, so that all that was required was to find a capital partner, and with inventory and tooling available, that didn't take much. Simon and Jan went on to develop more new products, as you shall hear later.

7

BUILDING DREAMS

In 1947, I was in a unique position. I had no immediate obligations, and was possessed of a respectable sum of money. I was at last a true capitalist, but no enterprises of great pitch and moment were in the offing. Rose and I decided to take an extended vacation, a luxury which had long been denied us. Some of our friends, such as Vera Shea and Henry Mancini, had moved to California, so we elected to spend five or six weeks soaking up the sun and playing golf.

Things had changed since my visit of a decade earlier. The landscape of Los Angeles had not yet been completely vandalized by inept architects. The Westin Company had developed the prime areas of Santa Monica, Brentwood and Malibu, but Beverly Hills retained a certain amount of elegance.

I sensed a new energy and activity. Gone was the narcissism of the past. There was an air of anticipation as all of those youngsters returning from the Pacific war theater settled in

California rather than going back to International Falls, Minnesota, or Dubuque, Iowa, or Broken Axle, Wyoming. They preferred the warm sun to the freezing weather. The population in California would expand, and real estate values would soar as the Veterans Administration made very low cost housing loans available. The building industry was in for a ride on a rocket.

During the war, whenever people traveled from coast to coast, there was a seven-hour stopover when the Twentieth Century Limited arrived in Chicago. While waiting for the Super Chief to take them the rest of the way to Los Angeles, regular tripsters would meet in the Pump Room of the Ambassador West Hotel. The doyenne of that table was Sis Willner, a breezy society columnist and a dear friend of mine; she wrote under the *nom de plume* Dorothy Dearborn. The attendees at her table included famous directors and producers, playwrights and novelists.

I remember one particular occasion when the most wonderful put-down befell me at the hands of the illustrious Carl Sandburg. During a lull in the spirited and amusing conversation, Sis turned to Carl and said, "You know, Charles was the youngest bridge player ever to play in the Eastern Championship. He was only fifteen when he played against Culbertson and Sidney Lenz." This scarcely raised an eyebrow, so Sis then announced that I was also one of the best amateur golfers in the New York metropolitan area. After a moment of bemused silence, Sandburg turned that wonderful craggy face toward me and said, "Young man, you seem to do nothing better than anyone I have ever met." After that, I was grateful for the fact that Sis shut up.

Sis later became enamored of a very attractive chap, Phil Philbin, a financier whose principal claim to fame was that he became the first victim of the SEC for a technical infraction of Joe Kennedy's new rules. Today he would be canonized. Happily, Phil was unscarred by this silly event, and he had the charming habit, when meeting someone for the first time, of saying, "Hello, I'm Phil Philbin. I've been in the can." Because of this forthright manner and Sis's determined personality, Phil was accepted everywhere.

When Sis and Phil married they bought the pool house to William Randolph Hearst's estate on Beverly Drive in Beverly Hills. It was a huge place, complete with its own pool, and was as beautiful and flawless as the Taj Mahal.

One day, in 1948, Phil asked me a direct question, the answer to which I would normally have fudged: "Can you write a check for $25,000 to the treasurer of the United States?" In shock, I found myself answering, "Maybe. Why?" He continued, "My financial backer has disappeared in a cloud of dust, and I need you to meet me at my lawyer's office. If you love Sis, you will do this for me." With that appeal, I was unable to take evasive action.

I made my way through the traffic to downtown Los Angeles, and entered a room in the law offices of Loeb & Loeb which was covered from corner to corner with blueprints. As I walked in the door, Phil proudly pointed at the drawings and said, "This is Camp Anza."

At the war's end the government, through the General Services Administration, had begun to sell all of the surplus materiel that had been acquired over the previous years. That meant land, buildings, tanks, guns, aircraft, trucks, and everything imaginable. Camp Anza had been a final departure point for young men bound for the campaign in China, Burma and India. Anza covered nineteen hundred acres, with a lake, a water system, a telephone exchange, and a plant to process sewage. As an experiment, instead of breaking it up into numerous small parcels, the government was going to try to sell it in a single package, including barracks and officers' club, extra work basins, and tons of soap.

A major real estate figure in San Francisco had expressed an interest in the land and therefore sent a functionary down to represent him, giving him a maximum figure to bid which had been tacitly agreed upon with the government.

Wandering around the sunny palm-lined streets of Riverside on the day of the auction was a local scoutmaster named Schmidt, who wanted to be a part of this major local event, if only as a spectator. There was one small catch: in order to keep the curiosity seekers from overflowing the auction room at the Mission Inn, one had to deposit a check for $2,500 to demonstrate financial stability. Knowing that the check would be returned after the auction, and being possessed of a bank account in the amount of $2,900, Mr. Schmidt, with a fine flourish, wrote a check for $2,500.

Although the bidding was not initially spirited, a few optimists in the crowd made some tentative bids and finally the tension mounted. There was excitement as a major bidder called from the back of the room: "$500,000!" Mr. Schmidt was so caught up in the excitement and so certain that the bidding would continue, that he bid $510,000. He was confident that an eager voice would follow his.

Unhappily, the emissary from the San Francisco real estate tycoon had only been authorized to bid up to $500,000. The auctioneer very properly did not give him time to call his principal and therefore, at the stroke of the hammer, Mr. Schmidt was the successful bidder at $510,000. That was exactly $507,100 more than he had in the world. He was stunned, but so thrown off balance that he signed the necessary papers and stumbled out into the sunshine.

There he met Phil Philbin, who told him to take it easy; he

would take over the bid. The Boy Scout leader gratefully accepted Phil's check for $2,500 and escaped with a prayer of thanks on his lips. The point was, however, that Phil didn't have any money either.

Phil then called me to the rescue. I didn't know anything about real estate, but I promised Phil I would see what I could do. On the day following my visit to Loeb and Loeb, I attended a board meeting of another company. I leaned over to my friend Harold, who did own some real estate, and politely inquired as to whether he had $12,500 that he never wanted to see again. I assured him that I would add $12,500 and we would take part in a real estate venture of giant proportions, in either direction. He immediately proved that I was not the only optimist in the world by saying yes. I gave him a check for $12,500, and asked that he go down to look at the property with Phil. If he thought it looked promising he would give Phil the checks on our behalf. I also knew that once Phil got his hands on him, he would be permanently separated from his boodle.

Within forty-eight hours of my return to New York, I received a call from Phil Philbin, who confessed that his arrangement with the government for payment actually contemplated an initial down payment of $102,500. The Federal government had given him seventy-two hours to come up with the opening deposit and told him that we should be prepared to close forthwith.

The matter was in the hands of the War Assets Administration in the person of Jess Larsen, who was in charge of the disposition of surplus property. I knew Tom Clark, the attorney general, quite well, and he arranged a meeting between Mr. Larsen and Nat Mendelson, my financial vice-president. Larsen brusquely advised Mendelson to have a check for $102,500 by noon the next day, along with a firm closing date, and the source of funds in writing. I called Harold, who agreed to put up the balance of the money, and we became the proprietors of what was to be named the Anza Realty Company. We distributed the stock between us: I took forty percent, Charlie Allen got forty, our attorney took fifteen, and Phil took the remainder.

Since we were now thinking about serious money, I felt it might be useful if I at least saw our property before it was confiscated. I prepared the check and arranged to deliver funds to the authorities, and took off for California to visit my new domain.

To a city boy, the vastness of nineteen hundred acres was overwhelming, but it looked like an abandoned mining town in the Northwest Territories. The grass had grown to knee length and above, and since the cost of hiring a local farmer to come in there and cut it was quite considerable, we arranged for a sheepherder to let loose his flock on our property. The results were miraculous. We not only had a well-manicured landscape, but also some pleasantly fat sheep, which were returned to their owner.

Anza consisted of some barracks, an officers' club, loading platforms for railroads, and an eight-mile connecting railroad to the Southern Pacific Railroad. We ultimately built twenty-five hundred houses on that property which were each just under one thousand square feet in area, and included designs by such famous architects as Richard Neutra, Marcel Breuer, Walter Gropius, and Mies van der Rohe. Houses that we sold then at $7500 have since sold for as much as $100,000.

The connecting line railroad was organized as a separate entity, and my son Philip, aged four, was duly elected president of the railroad without an opposing vote. One night, one of the country's top railroad executives came to our home for dinner, and he asked Philip what he wanted to be when he grew up. Instead of saying a baseball player or fireman, Philip announced,

"Chairman of the board!" He then advised our visitor that our railroad might not be as long as the New York Central, but it was just as wide.

A shopping center was built; we developed and improved the water system, and sold it eventually to the city of Riverside. We did a similar transaction with the sewage treatment plant. I had been careful to change the name of the sewage plant to the Anza Utility Company, lest some friend asked my kids what their father did and have them reply that he was chairman of a sewage company.

Phil Philbin was a charming fellow, but he was a rogue who had to be watched with great caution. The first time Rose and I visited Beverly Hills together we stayed at a hotel, but Phil and Sis were adamant that we be their guests in their beautiful home. They threw huge parties and the Steinway piano in the living-room would ring out tunes for the amusement of many well-known directors and stars. But all was not well in the camp. One afternoon, as Rose and I were on our way out, Rose asked me, "Do you know if Sis has any cash? I had to lend her twenty bucks today." I thought that maybe there was some family money, but I decided to ask Phil how he was set. "Well," he replied, "I suppose I could use fifty dollars." I reached in my pocket and gave him the money.

A couple of nights later, the four of us went to play cards at the home of the renowned Hungarian designer Marishka. The director and actor Don Wilson was also in attendance. I partnered Phil, who was not a good player, and by the end of the evening we had lost a substantial amount of money. Phil drew me aside and said, "Look, I don't have any cash on me, can you help out?" So I settled our debt and we all went home.

As we were having a sandwich in the kitchen before going to bed, Phil said, "Sis had to give a check for her losses tonight." There was an uncomfortable pause before he continued, "She doesn't have the money to cover it. Neither do I, so . . . " By the time we left their home, we had paid off their maid and cook, and watched as the Steinway, which was on approval, was taken back to the store.

Phil, unfortunately, was not above trying a little sleight of hand in business either. When we were putting the Anza deal together he tried to tell me that Nat Mendelson was creating an awkward atmosphere in the WASPish fields of Riverside and he wanted Nat out of the picture. Phil just didn't want anyone looking over his shoulder as he tried to do some of his own "creative" financing with the corporation's money. I ended up having to buy out Phil's five percent of the stock and send him on his way.

While the negotiations for Anza were being completed, I made my first contact with California politics. My company, General Panel, was building pre-fabricated houses at marginal cost; the local real estate board, however, objected to this strategy and asked us to desist.

We had taken out a loan from the Federal Housing Authority, so the government, in the shape of the Reconstruction Finance Committee, was the paying agent against our bills of lading. The appropriately named Hector Hate, who ran the RFC's California office, began to stall on payments, so we were stuck with picking up the mortgage payments. When I asked him why he wasn't observing the rules, Hate calmly explained that he had no confidence in our bookkeeping. However, for an annual fee of only $60,000, he had a friend who could fix that.

I immediately went to see State Senator Helen Gahagan Douglas and explained the situation, but she was unable to help me; she recommended I try a congressman in Whittier by the name of Richard Nixon. I arranged to meet with Nixon and his aide, Murray Chotiner. After lunch, during which Nixon struck me as being very shifty, Chotiner asked me to step out for a private conversation. He came straight to the point: "What's in it for the Congressman?" I said, "The opportunity to serve the people." Chotiner said, "I don't mean that." I snapped back, "I know what you mean, but you don't mean me. I'm not in that business." I left forthwith.

Years later, I was having lunch in the Four Seasons and I saw Pete Peterson, who was then Secretary of Commerce to President Nixon. Pete was one of the earliest directors of IMC Magnetics, so we knew each other well. We have occasionally divergent points of view, but that is just fine. He said, "The President is going to invite about half a dozen people to lunch at the White House. He wants to talk about his economic programs." This was before Nixon's disastrous decision to devalue the currency. I said, "Peter, the food at the White House is pretty lousy, and I don't want to sit in a room where I don't have the privilege of asking what might be embarrassing questions. So, since we are friends and I don't want to embarrass you, I'll pass." Pete said, "It's a shirt-sleeve meeting and you can say anything you like." So I went.

When I got into the White House, there were six men I knew; among them was Bill Renchard, Chairman of Chemical Bank. I was not a friend, but I was on the international board of ChemBank, so we knew each other quite well. Also present was the chairman of Standard Oil of Indiana and the chairman of Dow Chemical. They were all men who, in addition to running a business, had a sense of public responsibility and took part in major policy questions. We were all ardently agreed that Nixon was barking up the wrong tree.

The President's economic advisor, Paul MacCracken, came in followed by the President, who was very informal in a boyish way. Nixon said "I really want to know how you think I'm doing. Are things going the way they should?" To my astonishment, all of these men who had been expressing their disapproval to me a few minutes earlier, suddenly started to say things like, "Mr. President, I think you are doing just fine," and "I think you are definitely on the right track."

Now Nixon looked over at me, and I took a deep breath. I didn't want to embarrass Peter, but I knew I had to say what I really thought. "Mr. President, this is the most terrifying prospect: if you put phase two into action, within thirty days you will not be able to exchange American currency in Europe." There was a strained silence at the table, and although some of the others muttered vague comments of agreement, I knew I'd never get invited to the Nixon White House again. In all honesty, I can say that this prospect upset me not in the least.

Nixon was the same slippery customer I had met over twenty years earlier. As much as I disliked him, I had voted for him in 1972, only because the Democrats ran McGovern. My reasoning was that it is easier to handle a crook than a fool.

After my success with Anza, we set up a company to develop thirty-six thousand acres around the Salton Sea, just south of

Palm Springs. We sold the land in reasonably priced lots to about a hundred developers, who then built up the area and brought in utilities. It was a very successful arrangement.

I was spending a lot of time in Southern California and would go into Los Angeles to catch the returning flights to New York. I would stay at the Beverly Hills Hotel, which was owned by my friend Ben Silberstein. I would often arrive unshaven, still in my work clothes, and usually without a reservation. This infuriated the guys behind the desk, but with a prearranged signal they would slip me a key to an apartment.

On one occasion, the hotel was particularly busy, but I managed to obtain a beautiful five-room suite. It was decorated with enough flowers to put Campbell's funeral parlor to shame, and the tables were loaded down with bottles of liquor, hors d'œuvres, and caviar. On one of the larger bunches of flowers was a card that read, "Welcome, Bill Hearst." I opened the liquor and snacked on caviar, and when the bell-boy came up I said, "Go down and tell the manager, I now know how you treat the people you want."

During the one of these frequent trips to California, Rose and I saw that the home of child star Jane Withers was up for sale. In the thirties, Jane had rivaled Shirley Temple for the status of most popular movie munchkin, but her career was short-lived. Oddly enough, she is best remembered for her portrayal of Josephine the Plumber in a series of television commercials. Jane's house and grounds occupied eight acres on Sunset Boulevard, land today worth perhaps $20 million. It included such absolute necessities as a soda fountain and a hairdressing parlor. In the event of nuclear war, there was a fully-stocked bomb shelter.

I could have purchased this for an incredibly small amount of money, and I assured my wife that if she would like to live in

California, I could sell off one acre in five years for the cost of the entire house; we could pay for everything and be very wealthy in ten years. I said, "I have no reason to go back into the stock option business, and I don't particularly want to go into real estate; but I think we could make a go of it." It did not take her long to respond: "If you're telling me that you are going to move here, that is one thing. If you're asking my opinion, I agree with Joe Frisco. The scenery is great, but the cast is lousy." Miss Withers' house remained on the market.

I sometimes try to imagine what my life would have been like if I had bought the house and moved West. I can't. Every time I visit L.A. on business, I find it to be a city so much in the control of guilty, rich, young activists and loonies, that as I leave, I daren't look back lest I turn to salt and wind up in somebody's chicken salad.

The modern decline of Los Angeles can be symbolized by the palm trees which proliferate along every street. The palm is not indigenous to California; it is an imported species with shallow roots. Left unattended, it begins to flop over and adds to what is already decaying. Likewise, the people who came to live in Los Angeles always had in the back of their minds the expectation that they would one day pack their bags and get out of town. The structures they built were impermanent by New York standards, and soon exhibited a paint-peeling ugliness.

The violence in New York City is certainly very unpleasant and dangerous, but it is infinitely more menacing in Los Angeles, where the enormity of the city creates an unmanageable situation. This is emphasized and magnified by the fact that the huge wealth that exists there wasn't acquired in the traditional way. It came very quickly with the burgeoning industries of movies, oil, and high technology. California has not yet learned the responsibility of money.

✧ ✧ ✧

One of the more exotic deals I essayed in real estate involved my foray into the hospitality industry.

In the early sixties everybody began to talk about the leisure communities; in the decades to come, people would retire before they were forty and live the good life. This sounded fine to me, and an opportunity arose through Lindsay Hopkins, chairman of the executive committee of Coca-Cola. Hopkins came from a very rich Georgia family which owned the remnants of Carl G. Fisher Co. Prior to the Crash, Carl G. Fisher had developed Miami, but in one of the biggest bankruptcies in the history of the world, they lost everything except for nineteen hundred acres in the Bahamas, with one charming little sixty-five-room hotel.

I got the idea that I would like to own several such hotels. I had enough of a camp following to get started with a public auction, and I could use that paper to buy hotels in various other locations. I'd take a penthouse in every one of them, and Rose and I would spend the rest of our lives traveling around the world, having our own place to stay wherever we went.

I established a market as Hemisphere Hotels. I bought a golf course from Bob Hope in exchange for stock, and purchased a hotel in Martinique. I went to Berne, Switzerland to negotiate for the building of a beautiful hotel that, among other things, would have floating two-room suites made by Chris-Craft. One of the greatest landscape architects in the world was going to develop a jungle environment with channels and waterways, and there was to be a Hawaiian restaurant. Unfortunately, the local Prime Minister was a crook. Every time I brought in an engineer from Bechtel to see how the construction was going, it cost me twenty-five grand a minute. It finally failed because we just ran out of money. Bob Caverly, who had built the Hilton chain, came down to see if he could rescue the venture, but it was too late. The hotel was beyond fiscal salvation.

But even failure can have a silver lining; in this case, a painting by Pierre Bonnard. I knew one of the great art buyers in France. Heinz had been a refugee from Hitler's Germany and came to Paris with only fifty francs in his pocket. He was a brilliant dealer and he opened a gallery which grew into a giant fortune, with millions of dollars worth of great art. I was in Paris at the time we were doing the public offering for the hotel. It was a hot stock, and Heinz, who would gamble on anything, had picked up just under three thousand shares, but he was hungry for more.

He had a marvelous Pierre Bonnard which caught my attention. I said "Heinz, tell you what I'll do; I'll give you thirty thousand cash and the rest in Hemisphere stock." That's what we did.

Of course, the stock went to zip, but I got a Bonnard for thirty grand.

8

WALL STREET ENCORE

I returned to Wall Street in 1948 as master of my own firm. This time I had financial resources, and my interest was in venture capital banking. I had a practical knowledge of engineering and had successfully managed and developed a modern corporation. I now knew something of the technologies that were available to be integrated into our society.

I purchased a seat on the New York Stock Exchange for $168,000 and soon formed a firm with a skillful trader, my only other partner. Our trading success afforded me the time to pursue new ventures, whether on the floor of the exchange, or in capital markets arranging financing for the new companies springing up.

I had originally started as a specialist because as a floor broker I was just a glorified clerk. Trading in stocks by watching the tape and investing money was something that would nail you to the floor; you couldn't take your eyes off those fluctuating numbers. I realized, looking at the floor from the other side, that the strings were pulled from upstairs. No activity on the floor could engage my attention for long other than specializing.

Being a specialist firm in the fifties had certain advantages. We were like jockeys; we would ride whatever horse was assigned to us. All through the decade we played a tax game, and never made a dollar in short term. The law says that if you buy stock and sell it within twenty-nine days, it's a short term loss. If you sell in thirty days or more, it's a long term loss. The difference in tax is substantial. In addition, since a specialist was regarded as a dealer, I could charge all of my stock losses against my commissions. I knew that each stock would develop a certain amount of commission business during the course of a year. A moderately good stock would mean fifty thousand dollars a year; a very good stock might be three hundred thousand a year. I would count my stocks, estimate the commissions and come up with a number like, say, a million dollars. Now I knew that I could safely lose a million dollars in trading and break even. If you know that the worst you'll do is break even, that gives you a certain amount of confidence in trading and makes you take a little bit of a risk. That appealed to me. But you couldn't just go out and specialize; it had to be authorized by the Stock Exchange under very specific conditions. It was only open to excellent brokers whom they considered above average because you could easily get wiped out.

During the summers, Rose and I would take the children to a house near the beach in Cedarhurst, Long Island. Our near neighbors were Rose's close friend and fellow Ziegfeld chorine, Joyce Matthews and her husband, Milton Berle. Milton was then the unrivaled king of television with his "Texaco Star Theater," and the lady whose house Mr. Television had rented felt as if God had recognized her virtues; she made a practice of visiting two or three times a week at the least excuse.

I first met Milton casually in the thirties, but it was not until 1941 that Joyce, who was on-stage with Rose in *High Kickers*, formally saw to it that we became friends. In fact, Rose and I were so close to Joyce and Milton that we were present at the battle royal preceding their first divorce, and accompanied them on their second honeymoon in 1949. We remain close chums to this day.

Milton was born on Morningside Heights, a stretch of bucolic streets running alongside Morningside Park which, though not a major park, nonetheless gave the area a halcyon feeling. His mother, Sandra Berlinger, was a department store detective, and a very formidable lady indeed. Her vision for her son's theatrical career must have been prenatal. Almost as soon as Milton could speak, he was mugging and saying funny things. At the tender age of six, Milton found himself in a children's take-off on the Floradora Sextet, a very popular turn-of-the-century group.

During weeks of rehearsal the director had drubbed into the kids' minds that, as soon as the band struck up, they were to go on stage and start the dance routine with the right foot. On opening night, Sandra took Miltie aside and said, "Miltie, you start on the left foot." Miltie said, "But Mom, they told us to start on the right!" She said, "That's correct, but when you start on the left, nobody will notice anybody else." When the curtain rose, Milton started on his left foot, and the audience dissolved in laughter. For the entire run, Milton started on his left foot.

The local candy store in Miltie's neighborhood was run by a kindly old gentleman named Wagner. The kids managed to get some free candy and an occasional plain soda while enjoying each other's companionship in the warmth of the store. Wagner was not exactly a fashion plate and, from time to time, he was a little absent-minded. He would occasionally omit the formality of buttoning his fly (in those days it was buttons and not a zipper), which sent the local youngsters into gales of laughter, and was a source of comic relief in the neighborhood.

When Milton was about nineteen, he achieved the definitive goal. He was playing the Palace. His appearance featured him coming on stage wearing a pork pie hat, the brim pushed upward, and a raccoon coat. The leader struck up the band, the curtain rose. Milton strode to the center of the stage. He raised his eyes to the gallery gods, his arms waving in triumph, at which moment the raccoon coat opened, and the audience screamed with laughter. He stood transfixed in puzzlement. Sandra, sitting in the front row of the balcony, spotted the problem immediately. Milton's fly was open. But how could she impart the information to him? After a moment's hesitation, she stood up and, in a voice like a foghorn, bellowed: "Miltie, Miltie, WAGNER!" He got the message, did a half turn, and adjusted his pants.

Mr. Wagner's son, Leonard, became one of the most beloved and famous members of the New York Stock Exchange, a senior partner in the firm of Wagner Stott and Company.

During Milton's reign as Mr. Television, it was our practice on Tuesday evenings to sit in the audience of the Texaco show with Joyce. After the live performance, we would assemble at Lindy's with Henny Youngman, Jack Carter, Buddy Hackett, Red Buttons, Jan Murray, virtually all the stand-up comics in New York; they would occupy a table in the front of the room with the express purpose of making one another laugh, which is no easy task when everyone knows each other's jokes. Rose and I would relish watching each comic trying to top the other.

Milton Berle, Rose and Charles

Jack Carter had a zany sense of humor, which worked better in an informal environment than on stage or screen. There was a radio personality by the name of Martin Block, who hosted a television program called "The Make-Believe Ballroom." His occasional appearances at Lindy's gave the word "bore" a bad name. One evening, he tried to put the table to sleep by droning endlessly about his new Rolls-Royce. When Martin stopped to take a breath, Jack began reminiscing, "When I was a kid, our first car was a big yellow Charlton Heston. It had four forward speeds and running boards, but it was not large enough to accommodate our growing family, so we traded it in for a Liberace. The Liberace was fancy but did not really have enough power and after a little while we switched to a Mercedes McCambridge. This lasted until we finally bought a Fazenda." (Louise Fazenda was an old time movie star.)

Swifty Morgan was an enigmatic character who, if he did not exist, could not be imagined. He spoke in a unique form of fractured English. For example, encouraging a friend to see a Broadway show, he said, "Don't miss it if you can." Another of his mangled expressions was, "I never liked him and I always will." His activities included selling neckties from a small suitcase to some of the most powerful people in New York or Hollywood, who treated him in a friendly fashion. Swifty's most Runyonesque claim was that he had written a book called *How to Cheat at Polo*.

Milton, of course, more than held his own at Lindy's. He had a memory that was nothing less than a joke file. When we were together, I would snap out a category, such as "dentists," and Milton would immediately rattle off a string of jokes on that subject. He was also a master of the put-down. In 1968, when his daughter Victoria married James Nokes of Rosenberg, Texas, Miltie told Rose, who was at the wedding, "I would have preferred it if it had been James Rosenberg from Nokes, Texas."

Musical and variety stars were frequent visitors at Miltie's; whenever I was around, I always seemed to be running into Adolph Green, Nan Wynn, or Georgie Gibbs. There was one memorable occasion when Sammy Fain was supervising the recording of the love song he wrote for Bill Holden's film, *The World of Suzie Wong*. The great Lauritz Melchior was giving it his all in the studio and hit a particularly splendid high note. As the rafters shook, Sammy turned to us all and said, with a wicked grin of pride, "I wrote that note!" Milton was even adept at manufacturing stars. During an engagement at the Carnival nightclub, Milton invited our Swedish cleaning lady, Svea, to see the show and arranged for her to be seated at a table with Ed Sullivan. At the end of the show, as was his custom, Milton introduced the celebrities present in the house. When Ed Sullivan was announced, Milton raised his hand to silence the applause and said, "Ladies and gentlemen, it is my extreme pleasure to introduce to you now that great Swedish motion picture star, Svea Johnson!" The spotlights instantly found her, and she stood up, nodding and waving her hand. The audience went wild. For one shining moment, Svea was a star.

Milton was, and remains to this day, a dear friend. He has always been a great favorite with our older children, Philip and John: they still inquire to this day how "Uncle Miltie," an accomplished magician with a particular facility for card tricks, bamboozled them with one particularly dazzling trick, and I can do nothing to elucidate. Milton is no help: he claims to be able to do the trick solely through the intervention of the supernatural. Thanks to programs like A&E's "Biography" and the resurgence of interest in the Golden Age of Television, many people can now enjoy Miltie at his prime. But I was fortunate to be there live.

Joyce Matthews' next husband also played a substantial role in my life. He was Billy Rose, the showman and legendary impresario. Though I had met him casually during my association with Bernard Baruch in the thirties, it was not until Joyce and my wife conspired to bring their husbands together that I got to know him. We were a spectacularly unlikely pair and, at first, I did not relate to him at all. Flamboyantly show biz, always on a honeymoon with his mirror, he would constantly say or do things that set my teeth on edge.

For his part, Billy wasn't sure what to make of me. We were like two fighters circling a ring and he decided to test my mettle. One evening, Billy, Joyce, Rose, and I were on our way to dinner at Jack Small's house in New Jersey (he ran the Shubert empire with John Shubert) when Billy suddenly asked what was happening with Western Union. He had found out that I was peripherally involved in a deal for the stock. "Is it true they are going to raise the dividend and split the stock?" he asked. I confirmed this impression and thought nothing more of it. The next day, Billy called me at my office and repudiated my information, based on a "reliable" report from a mutual acquaintance who had just met with Western Union's president in New York. The meeting to perform the stock split was to take place in California, so I said, "Your friend must have long feet. He's on the coast right now." Billy silently retreated. Two days later he called back and admitted, "You're right, that guy is dead." The transaction took place as planned and I had passed Billy's test. If I hadn't known how many shares were outstanding or what the earnings were, he would not have trusted me. That kind of challenge from a friend does not sit well with me.

Billy thought he had acquired a taste for great art. I accompanied him to a gallery where he walked around selecting several small but exquisite paintings by Rembrandt, Hals, and Velasquez. After he had made his choices he asked the gallery owner the cost of the pieces and was quoted a figure in the region of seven hundred thousand dollars. Billy snorted, "I'll give you three hundred thousand. Cash!" The gallery owner tried to reason, but Billy was adamant, and after some heated exchanges we left, *sans* paintings. A few months later, the gallery called and, to Billy's glee, accepted the offer.

That transaction offended me: I don't like to see Art cheapened by Commerce. My ability to enjoy a painting diminishes in direct proportion to my knowledge of its monetary value. Billy felt the exact opposite, as he proved on more than one occasion.

But somewhere along the line, a miracle happened. He developed both true passion and cultivated taste. As his wealth grew, he bought antique furniture and paintings and learned a great deal about them. Having purchased a Rembrandt, he very soon learned more about the Dutch master than had Mrs. Rembrandt. So it was with Matisse, Rodin, English drawing room furniture, and Paul Storr silver. He was impressed with my knowledge of eighteenth-century furniture and paintings, as well as Oriental carpets, and this formed the basis for our tenuous friendship. Billy's possessions had civilized him.

If there was one thing at which Billy excelled, it was thinking big. Like Napoleon, Alexander, and other short men of history, his dreams were boundless, and his ability to conceptualize vast enterprises was nothing short of astonishing. His great financial success did not begin with his writing of such songs as "Barney Google," "I Found a Million Dollar Baby in a Five and Ten Cent Store," "Me and My Shadow," and "Teach Me Tonight." Nor, indeed, did his nightclub ventures result in his building a great fortune. His production of "Jumbo with Jimmy Durante plus Elephants" cost Jock Whitney millions; it netted Billy nothing. (It did, however, provide the occasion for a famous quip. Two stagehands approached Durante and asked him, "Where are you going with that elephant?" Jimmy innocently asked, "What elephant?")

Billy first climbed to the top of the monetary mountain by producing the Aquacade in Fort Worth, Texas, followed by a similar opus in Ohio. Finally, at the 1939 World's Fair in New York, the showman, dubbed the Bantam Barnum, struck the mother lode with Eleanor Holm. Eleanor was one of the most beautiful girls of her time, a world champion swimmer, and Billy's second wife. She was made doubly famous by the nuttiness of Avery Brundage, the panjandrum of the American Olympic Committee, who suspended her from the 1936 Olympic Games in Berlin for the trivial offense of drinking a glass of champagne while en route to Europe. Since Eleanor was a darling of the public, Mr. Brundage did not endear himself to her fans who were interested in America's performance.

There resulted weeks of titilating newspaper stories and pictures of Eleanor in fetching bathing suits.

Eleanor became the centerpiece of Billy Rose's Aquacade, which Billy had charmed the Chemical Bank and the City of New York into building. Here she was surrounded with thirty or more other aquatic beauties and a group of suitably handsome young men. They presented water ballets that were the precursors of Esther Williams' performances in the movies. It was a visual feast and easily the most popular and profitable diversion offered at the World's Fair.

Under the conditions of Billy's deal with Grover Whalen, official greeter of the City of New York, and thanks to the generosity of Chemical Bank, Billy invested exactly nothing in this structure, having correctly sold the city the idea that it would become a permanent public pool available to people in Flushing.

With minimal capital invested, and only the labor needed to collect one dollar per person for eight shows a day, he had a money machine. Each performance filled the ten thousand-seat stadium to the rafters; at $80,000 a day, Billy's fortunes skyrocketed, and with the sage advice of Barney Baruch, the money was wisely invested and grew splendidly. Much of his investment was in real estate: Billy was the only bachelor I knew who had an island with a forty room "cabin," a forty-six room private house on 93rd between Park and Madison in New York, and a fourteen room estate in Jamaica.

Billy and Joyce later owned a very beautiful estate in northern Westchester County. Rose and I were frequent weekend visitors to the lush acres at Mount Kisco, as were Noël Coward, Ralph Bunche, Deems Taylor, Adlai Stevenson, Marlene Dietrich, and a passel of other lively and fascinating characters. In April of 1956, after Rose and I returned from California on the

Super Chief, we were shocked to read that, because of a short circuit in the electrical system, Billy's magnificent house had burned to the ground the previous Sunday night. Priceless art and furniture were lost to the world. The only occupants of the house at the time were the butler and three servants, but the fire spread rapidly. The butler was able to salvage only a large Grant Wood painting and a brass cannon, leaving behind priceless examples of Velasquez, Rembrandt, Renoir, Matisse, and some great English furniture. We were crushed on reading the news, but made a note that the best kind of butler to employ would be an art critic.

I immediately called Billy in his New York apartment, and it was then that Billy Rose became my friend for life. After hearing me express my regrets for his tremendous loss, he calmly said: "Listen, kiddo, I didn't catch cancer and nobody was hurt. I will buy more paintings and more furniture and forget this fire. Thank you for your kind words." I don't know anyone else who would have that sense of values after such a catastrophic event.

Billy obviously wanted another house, but his thoughts now centered more on a town house in Manhattan. One evening he was having dinner with Ruth and Augustus Goetz, the playwrights who had such a success in 1954 with *The Immoralist*. They excitedly announced that they had just seen the ideal house, a forty-six room mansion on 93rd Street between Madison and Park Avenues. It had an eighty-foot front with a semicircular driveway. The house had been a gift from the legendary George Baker, chairman of the First National Bank, to his daughter Gloria when she married William Goadby Lowe. Mr. Baker's own house on the corner of 93rd Street and Park is the only structure with a station of the New York Central Railroad in its basement. When he traveled to Chicago, the Twentieth Century Limited stopped there for him.

Billy insisted on seeing the house immediately, but Ruth Goetz protested that it was unlikely that the lord of the manor would show the house at ten o'clock at night. Billy waved her off, saying, "Look, if he wants to sell the house, he won't care about the time." The party of three set off for the magnificent mansion. A sleepy-eyed caretaker answered the door with the information that the owner did not live there and suggested that Billy come back the next day. Billy countered that this fellow had better call the owner lest he incur his employer's wrath and be sent to the stocks.

Sure enough, the new owner, who had just bought the house at auction, put in an appearance. As Billy explained it to me, they arrived at a deal at four in the morning.

According to Billy, he had several conversations with the seller the next day, and they arranged for the lawyers and other functionaries to get together. Suddenly, Billy found it impossible to get this gent on the phone. He was enraged to read in *The New York Times* a few days later that the house had been sold to the Czechoslovakian government for their United Nations embassy. Billy declared war.

The next morning, in Thomas Dewey's office, Billy screamed that Czechoslovakia had invaded his territory, but Dewey explained that since it was a real estate transaction, there was nothing Billy could do legally to enforce their agreement. He did, however, make another suggestion.

He observed that it was highly unlikely that the Czech government would enjoy unpleasant publicity. Billy might make some mention of the transaction in his column, "Pitching Horseshoes," which appeared worldwide in about eighteen hundred publications. Dewey believed that it might bring some reaction. That did not begin to describe the ensuing events.

Wires buzzed from Prague to Washington and thence to

New York. Within forty-eight hours, there was no prospective Czechoslovakian embassy on 93rd Street. The enraged laird placed a Chinese curse on Billy and his ancestors. He refused to acknowledge that Billy Rose was alive and would accept no telephone calls or deals of any kind. So our hero was back to square one.

Again, Tom Dewey had a simple solution: "If you have a friend whose credit is good for that amount of money and who has no connection with show business, I suggest that you bid in his name."

That evening, Billy called me to announce that he had used my name in vain, and had made an offer on the house by telegram to Previews Inc., a real estate broker. As an afterthought, he asked me for the name of my bank so that the seller could check my financial status.

The next morning, George Texter, chairman of the Marine Midland Bank, called me to politely ask if I was in complete control of my faculties. I conceded that I was in the middle of one of the most outlandish and zany experiences in recent history, and was awaiting the outcome with bated breath.

Billy commenced a series of daily calls which kept me informed of the progress of the negotiations until, late one afternoon, he congratulated me, saying, "You are now the owner of a forty-six room townhouse."

I was asked to appear at the office of prominent attorney Louis Nizer, with a check to open an escrow. The amount involved was to be liquidated damages and reached six figures, so I thought it might be advisable to have some evidence in writing of Billy's intentions to purchase the house.

I instructed my lawyer to draw the necessary papers. He offered to have me committed to a nearby asylum at his own cost, but I defended myself by commenting that he, like all lawyers, was an alternate mass of ambition and inaction, while I was a man who probed the outer limits of the adventurous. Further, I pointed out that lawyers, when confronted with the unknown, prepared for the worst, while I prepared for the best.

Billy admonished me, on pain of the rack, to avoid any mention of his name at Nizer's office, but I knew Louis Nizer very well, and it was thus within the realm of probability that Nizer knew I was acquainted with Billy Rose. Very confidently, Billy told me that this matter would be handled by one of their junior partners and that Louis Nizer would never even appear on the scene. He proved to be right.

My instructions from Billy were clear and concise. "Give him anything he wants. I want the house." When we completed what passed for negotiations in this transaction, there was virtually nothing left but one forty-watt bulb. Not a single chandelier and, believe it or not, not one toilet seat remained. Each time they asked for something, I would assent with a fine, free, careless hand.

One of the conditions was that I could not transfer the contract. The seller was properly wary about the limits of Billy's reach. Therefore, unless Billy ultimately closed the deal, I would own a house or lose my deposit.

This was June, but for tax reasons the escrow was to close sometime in September. Immediately after the meetings at Nizer's office, Billy made the surprise announcement that he and Joyce were leaving for Poland and Russia on the morrow. For a time now, I would be the suzerain of a mansion. A few weeks later, I still had not heard from the flying Roses as they invaded the heartland of Communist Russia. My wife had a vision of the single engine airplane flying Billy and Joyce from Moscow to Warsaw making an unscheduled stop at the bottom of the Dnieper River. With that thought in mind, we decided to hie ourselves hence to what might soon be our ancestral mansion.

Arm in arm, we walked the half block from our Park Avenue abode to the new house. We entered what was surely one of the most overwhelming structures I had ever seen. The ceilings must have been fifteen feet high, and the living room was the size of the main dining room in the Plaza Hotel.

The sheer size of the rooms, however, was accentuated by the god-awful condition. In the main salon, antique Chinese wallpaper was peeling from the walls. The ceilings were cracked, and in the gloom the whole appearance was that of Wuthering Heights. In an effort to lower my wife's rising temperature, I pointed to the elegant winding staircase and said, "Gee, won't the kids look great sliding down the banister!"

Rose looked at me darkly and ordered, "Get me out of this mausoleum. If any of your hare-brained schemes include owning this house, you'll have to do it with someone else, so get out your little black book."

In mid-August, Billy finally returned and immediately called to announce that the closing would take place September 8th. I was requested to have a check ready for the event. I suggested that Billy should deliver to me a cashier's check for the entire amount so that I could deposit it in my bank for immediate credit. I also had my lawyer draw suitable papers memorializing the ultimate transaction intention, which I would appreciate Billy signing on that very day. Without comment, he agreed and thanked me for my forbearance.

The great day arrived. The seller, his attorneys, along with my own attorney and Billy's lawyer, present incognito, met in the kitchen of the Goadby Lowe house under the forty-watt bulb, and signed the documents. I received the key in exchange for the check, and the former owners' entourage departed. Billy's lawyer informed that Billy was waiting at his office in the Ziegfeld Theater for the transfer to be made immediately.

I explained that that would not be possible since I had an executive committee meeting on Long Island. Billy's representative recoiled in shock, "My God, what happens if you have an accident on the way out?" I grinned and said, "The same question occurred to my wife and myself while Billy was dashing around Russia like a fugitive evading the KGB. Sorry, but Billy will have to wait until tomorrow, 10:00 A.M."

At the house, the next day, the transfer was duly completed and there appeared on Billy's face a look that, for all the world, might have been the dreamy, far-away expression that Mount St. Helens had after its eruption had decimated several villages. He had won.

He then turned to me and innocently asked what we were doing on Friday evening, the 8th of February. I thought at first he was joking, but he was deadly serious. He was going to throw a housewarming party that evening, and was inviting just sixteen selected people. He wanted us to be present at the unveiling.

Having redecorated our apartment in something just under a century, I looked at Billy with some skepticism, but he confidently assured me that, on the designated night, he would have everything done in every room in the house, and every detail would be the quintessence of elegance and charm. I agreed to transmit his invitation to Rose and also to certify that it was not coerced.

Weeks flew by and Billy was flying with them, shuttling back and forth from Paris and London twice a week. He engaged a famous decorator to coordinate the colors and fabrics and to arrange for the making of draperies and other minor things that can bankrupt people of lesser wealth.

Finally, on Friday, February 8, 1957, Rose and I presented ourselves at precisely eight o'clock in front of the portals of Billy's new home. We arrived coincidentally with Jack and Edith Small. Jack was a strikingly funny man and a friend who, along with John Shubert, ran the great Shubert theater empire, so he was one of the most powerful men in the theater. One would never guess this because he was quite unassuming and completely untheatrical.

We rang the bell, and the doors were opened by the quintessence of elegance. There stood the clone of C. Aubrey Smith, six feet four inches tall, with a huge mane of white hair and a perfectly fitted white tie and tails. Billy had absconded with Fortune, Harry Luce's butler and aide-de-camp.

Billy had made a proposal to Fortune which was very difficult to refuse. First, he offered him a signing bonus, as popularized in the National Football League today. Second, he paid him a princely salary and deposited a sum in the bank which would vest with Fortune were he to stay with Billy for two years. It was a unique arrangement for the times, but, when Billy wanted something, he usually got it.

As we passed Fortune into the magnificent foyer, we encountered a breathtaking collection of sculptures by Rodin, Maillol, Zorach, Jean Arp, and Jacob Epstein. An exquisite Italian marble flooring was the foundation for two onyx columns.

Twenty feet behind Fortune's disappearing back stood the new seigneur, all five feet one-and-one-half inches of him, decked out in a newly tailored forest green smoking jacket. Evening trousers and pumps with bows completed the picture. He was positioned before a magnificent Chippendale fireplace over which was casually hung Sir Joshua Reynolds' famous portrait of *The Strawberry Girl.* Jack made a deliberate inventory of the scene before him, seeming to stop momentarily at a particular piece of art. After what seemed an eternity of indecision, Billy timidly said, "Well, Jack, what do you think?"

Jack's reply nearly sent me scurrying under the table. "Billy, if you were three inches taller, you would not have needed this house." I waited for the roof to fall in, but Billy knew Jack and understood that there was no malice in this comment.

We walked up the majestic staircase to the drawing room, which was like a visit to a Hapsburg Palace. It was magnificently eighteenth century with traditional English academy works by Gainsborough and Reynolds. It was a perfectly elegant setting, even down to the Chinese famille rose pieces, small exquisite sculptures and antique silver on the side tables. Billy had fulfilled his promise; all forty-six of the rooms were furnished to the last detail. He had imported Italian craftsmen to repair the ceilings, scoured the world for artisans to repair the ancient wallpaper, and emptied half the showrooms of the European antique dealers. It was a triumph.

Infinitely more gratifying was the cast at the evening festivities. I was relegated to the unfortunate position of settling for Marlene Dietrich as my dinner partner. She commented that in Europe sex was a fact; in America, a fetish. My wife had to endure the charms of Maurice Chevalier. Present also were Ralph Bunche, Lena Horne, Moss and Kitty Hart, and Richard and Dorothy Rodgers. My wife and I were the only civilians in attendance.

I would like to say that Marlene Dietrich was so immediately smitten by my ineffable charm that she shoved a perfumed kerchief in my hand, calling softly "Vladivostok, Vladivostok, follow me." That did not happen. Dietrich was, rather, the obverse of her movie image, a simple, unspoiled lady bubbling over with humor. She loved to cook and keep house, and talked about family. She could have talked about quantum physics for all I cared, because having her as a dinner partner was equivalent to winning the Irish sweepstakes.

For several years afterwards, when the Roses were at home, there was a Friday night dinner party for sixteen, and it was our great good fortune to frequently be included. To take part in the sparkling discussions or listen to some of the great artists perform was ample reward for my part in buying the house.

One of the many built-in luxuries at Billy's house was a gymnasium. Three mornings a week my wife would join Joyce in the gymnasium, where a muscular Irishman would torment them through a half-hour of exercise. There would then be a soothing and relaxing massage which made up for all of the pain. One day, while Rose was on the massage table, the door opened and she saw a face adorned by familiar, long mustachios. Billy introduced my wife to Salvador Dali.

In 1944, Billy had produced a musical revue entitled *The Seven Lively Arts*. With music by Cole Porter, sketches by Moss Hart and George Kaufman, a ballet section composed by Stravinsky, and a cast headed by Beatrice Lillie, Bert Lahr, and Benny Goodman, it should have been a huge success. The critics were less than kind, however, and the show was sinking fast. Billy was unchastened by the reviews and determined to keep the show running by whatever publicity stunts he could contrive. He considered an advertisement picturing a critic swinging from a gibbet, but didn't know which one to select.

A young Spanish painter had just arrived on the scene, and his provocative canvasses seemed to derive from De Chirico. His name was Salvador Dali. Billy convinced Dali that if he would paint his impressions of each of the seven lively arts, Billy would get him so much publicity that his works would immediately become candidates for display at the Metropolitan Museum. Dali fell for this tale and painted seven enormously imaginative pictures, each one about six feet in height, which were then placed in the back of the theater.

Life magazine actually did a seven-page spread of these paintings, and Billy's rather optimistic promise turned into reality as Dali's works reached a vast audience. They couldn't save the show, however, which closed after a decidedly *un*-lively five months. The paintings were relocated to the billiard room of Billy's home in Mt. Kisco. When the house was devastated by the fire, Dali's works unhappily were lost.

A few years later, Dali, who still had the original transparencies, told Billy he would like to do them over for him. Billy thanked him and offered to pay the $2,000 a canvas he had paid for the originals. "But that is impossible!" countered Dali. "I am world famous. I get $75,000 to $100,000 a canvas." Billy quietly reminded him that, while that was true, it was Billy who had given him his first great boost with the spread in *Life* magazine. After a pregnant Iberian silence, Dali said, "I will replace them."

The later works were infinitely better than the originals and were hung in Billy's new billiard room at the 93rd Street house. My wife met Dali when he came over with the truckers to deliver the paintings to Billy.

Billy invited me one night to play billiards and discuss the market. He owned stock in fifty-five different companies, and asked me, if I had to own only one stock, what it would be. I had recently done an analysis of American Telephone for my own benefit, and as the signs and portents were excellent, I recommended the stock without hesitation.

Next day, he announced he was going to sell every other stock, and as he developed the cash, send it to me with an order to buy AT&T. This was the genesis of Billy's becoming the largest individual shareholder of AT&T. Later, we bought New York Central Railroad and Pennsylvania Railroad shares. It all added up to a large fortune.

Despite Billy's great financial success, he thought poor. When he was a kid growing up in the Bronx, his father rarely worked more than twenty-six weeks a year and the family struggled. Although he now had a majestic fortune, Billy could not rid himself of the fear of losing the security that this gave him, and panicked at the thought of ever being poor again.

It was for this reason that Billy was never a contributor of any consequence to philanthropic causes. But in the latter part of his life, through Ben Hecht, an ardent Zionist, Billy became interested in the state of Israel. When the war broke out in 1956, a consortium of nine of us, including Ben, Billy, and myself, raised a half a million dollars and bought a tank! We gave it to the State of Israel through a charitable foundation and we took a tax deduction on it. Subsequently, Billy engaged the famed architect Noguchi to build the Billy Rose Sculpture Garden in Jerusalem. It was there that Billy wanted his extraordinary collection of great sculpture to rest, and it is now one of the premier attractions of Jerusalem.

Still, nothing took the place of New York. That was where geography began and ended for Billy. Once he traveled to Chicago with the sports writer Jimmy Cannon. Upon checking into his room, he was met with the muzzle of a .38-caliber gun. The face behind the gun instructed him to throw all his money and his wallet on the bed, to take off his watch and his ring, to lie down on the floor. Billy nervously complied, and then the unwelcome visitor said, "If you call out in less than five minutes, I'll come back and kill you." Billy paid careful attention, and it was five minutes and one second by his interior clock before he dared to cross the hall and tell Cannon what had happened. The sports writer was a pretty cool customer and, scowling, asked, "Why the hell didn't you call out?" Billy responded, "Anybody who leaves New York deserves what he gets."

✧ ✧ ✧

If the fifties seem in memory to have been smooth, placid, and relatively untroubled, I nonetheless vividly remember the one day that brought me to the brink of a familiar abyss.

Ike's heart attack struck on a Friday, so the news didn't become public until the Saturday. In the market, my first reaction to any event is to assume that people will respond emotionally and do the worst thing. My outfit was well capitalized, with about $12 million in equity (I personally never made less than a million and a half dollars per year during the mid-fifties), and we were a specialist firm so we were not borrowing much. When my partner (whom we shall call Bobby) called to ask for my prediction, I said, "It will be a mess. Who knows how much off the market will open on Monday?" Bobby fudged, and said, "Well, it's *Yom Kippur*, and I have to go to temple. Do whatever you think is best." I said, "It's your money, too, you know." "This is the only holy day I observe," he said. "I'll call you tomorrow."

In the meantime, I called business associates in Europe and Scotland for their perception of how world markets would be affected. When Bobby called me again, I had re-assessed my position: "I was wrong. It's not going to be a mess; it's going to be a catastrophe!" When the market opened on that Monday morning I was alone with three clerks to handle the transactions.

The market opened with such an avalanche of sales that the governors passed a rule that you could not open a stock more than two dollars down without their permission. But there was such chaos in the bidding that the market just wouldn't stop going down. Amid this confusion I got a call from Bobby. He asked, "How are things going?" I yelled at him, "It's wonderful! It's a walk in the park! Good-bye!" And I slammed the phone down. *Yom Kippur* or no, he left Woodmere, Long Island, and was on the floor within the hour.

The devastation was unspeakable. By the end of the day, every stock we had was open, and anything that we had sold had taken a beating. Worse, instead of having a surplus in capital, we now had a debit of $13 million, so all in all we were $25 million down.

It was 1929 deja vu. One more day like this and I'd either be on the lam to Acapulco or collecting unemployment. I stayed away from high windows as I tried desperately to formulate a strategy. Do we hold our position? Play the market short? Nothing sprang immediately to mind. No one knew how the President would fare or how the market might open the next day.

Tuesday morning dawned too soon. Minutes before the market opened, an uneasy silence reigned on the floor of the New York Stock Exchange; brokers waiting by their posts, eyes fixed on the tape which, at any minute, would explode into frenzied activity. Everybody at our post was looking to me — my partner, Bobby; our clerks — they were all waiting solemnly, like men on a landing craft ready to hit the beach.

I took a breath. "Whatever happens to Eisenhower I think there will be a slight recovery, however feeble. Most people will want to sell in the morning, but I think we should hold off." I took an even deeper breath. "Let's just keep all our positions."

By Tuesday afternoon, we had made all our money back; and on Wednesday morning, we found ourselves with a half-million dollar profit.

Sometimes I wonder where I'd be if on that one day I had guessed wrong.

❧

Charles & Continental Telephone Co. President Phillip Lucier upon first trading day of
Continental common stock on New York Stock Exchange trading floor

9

VENTURE CAPITALIST

There isn't a business school in the country which would counsel this, but the best advice I can give to a prospective investor is never underestimate the value of errors. Sometimes, making a mistake is the smartest thing you can do.

New businesses thrive and wither with startling alacrity, but if you learn when to quit, you will stay ahead of the game and live to fight another day. A new business has the same life expectancy as the Marlboro man peering into a tank of propane gas with a lighted cigarette dangling from his lips. It is, therefore, wise to be skeptical of vague prognoses and woolly perorations about the state of the economy; faith may be an admirable asset, but experience has taught me that doubt is what makes money.

I am a born contrarian. When the New York Giants baseball team was thirteen and a half games behind the Brooklyn Dodgers in 1951, there were only fifteen games left in the sea-son. I took twelve to one that the Giants would win the pennant and when Bobby Thompson hit the "shot that was heard around the world" I was proved right. Why did I make that wager? I didn't care if the Giants won the pennant; I just didn't believe that anything was a twelve to one bet.

I don't believe there is a solution for every problem in the world, but I do believe that for those problems that are solvable there is usually more than one solution. The obvious or probable solution is not necessarily the right one. The first appropriate solution you devise may be the least efficient. You have to discipline yourself to supposing that if it's wrong, you must seek other avenues. There is nothing that says that, having gotten an idea that is wrong, you're committed to it for the rest of your life.

I have always loved a challenge. I would rather work for nothing in an area that intrigues me than be paid handsomely for something that bores me. For many years I've made a habit of taking about an hour a day, closing my office door, and gazing at the ceiling. I think over the panoply of problems I am facing, and I engage each one in a test, discarding or accepting solutions as they occur to me. I didn't learn this way of conducting business at Harvard; this is just one of the valuable legacies of my mentor and friend Barney Baruch. I take an analytical position, but I accept that all solutions are susceptible to change. Flexibility is the password.

How I personally benefited from a potentially disastrous mistake is best demonstrated by the story of how Contel came into being. I had no idea at the time that the proposal that was brought to me would be any different from the ten other business proposals I receive each week.

I have always been interested in sports, and consider myself a big New York Giants football fan, as do my sons, John and

Randy. I knew Allie Sherman, the coach of the Giants, and also a couple of their famed stars, notably Frank Gifford and Kyle Rote. They were kind enough to allow my sons to watch practice sessions and to meet such fine players as Y. A. Tittle and Roosevelt Grier. I earned a lot of brownie points with my sons for this special treat. One day in 1960, Kyle introduced me to a friend whom I shall call Mr. Meadows. This gentleman owned a small telephone company in Alaska, and wondered if I could help to arrange $350,000 in financing. I agreed to inspect the balance sheet and business plan, and after looking over the prospective figures, estimated that approximately $1.5 million would be needed for the enterprise to have a chance for success.

Meadows looked at me pityingly and offered, "Don't you think I know I need $1.5 million? But if I can't get $350,000, how the hell am I going to get $1.5 million?" I counted to ten and proceeded, "Listen, I have been in the banking business most of my adult life, and I have never met anybody who had an unquenchable desire to lose $350,000. On the other hand, I know a lot of people who, either individually or collectively, would invest $1.5 million to make a good deal of money." Uncertainly, he queried, "Like whom?" I blushingly replied, "Like me. After all, it is my business."

According to Meadows, Stromberg Carlson Company, which is a division of General Dynamics, had done a feasibility study on extending the telephone exchange, and had agreed, upon the injection of adequate equity capital, to make a $2 million loan against the purchase of their equipment. My dear friend Sylvan was on the Executive Committee of General Dynamics, and he confirmed that Stromberg predicted a substantial growth in telephony in Alaska, with a possibility of great financial reward.

Other than AT&T, there were 4,650 telephone companies of varying sizes throughout the country. They ranged from eighty phones to a couple of million. American Telephone had wired America's cities, but rural America, with more than half the geographical area of the continental United States, was wired by so-called independent telephone companies. AT&T had an investment plan that rivaled that of some countries; they were firmly and conservatively entrenched. When you went to work for them you knew certain things: you never lost your job, and if you stayed for long enough, wore the right suit and tie, and didn't rock the boat, you became a junior executive. Thus it is with all bureaucracies.

After the Bell patents had expired in 1893, small groups in rural communities bought shares in the local phone company. Farmers would put up primitive telephone poles and string open "C" wire from one farm to the other. They would then employ a local woman to run the switchboard from the general store for a modest fee. And so the independent telephone industry came into being.

It was a sleepy little business that in most cases could not even connect with long-distance lines. On the other hand, if somebody was having a baby, or a veterinarian's services were required, the lady at the switchboard generally knew where everybody in town was at any moment of the day, and could contact them immediately.

This is the way things were until the Second World War came to an end. When Johnny came marching home, the Veterans Administration provided low-cost loans for housing, and construction was frenetic on what had been farmland, as wheat and corn fields magically became shopping centers amidst hundreds of ranch-type houses. It had been the order of the day for a young couple to live with the parents of the newlyweds. The telephone was not as widespread as it is nowadays; I remember when I was a youngster how we would jump when the phone rang. After the war, however, there was a burgeoning demand as young marrieds bought their own homes and wanted to be in easy contact with their neighbors.

In order to retain franchises, the small telcos had to serve the newcomers, which meant attracting investment capital. Many of the franchise owners lacked knowledge of finance and their limited access to money proved unequal to the task of building for the "baby boom."

Meanwhile, there might be crop failures, and a farmer might begin to owe the local doctor, veterinarian, or undertaker money which he could not pay. Being a good, solid, honorable American citizen, he would call his creditor and sell his share in the telephone company in lieu of payment. In this way, hundreds of doctors, veterinarians, and undertakers found themselves owning thirty percent of the phone companies, but as the traffic volume increased, it was necessary to build new telephone plants to accommodate this volume. Generally, the money was borrowed from a local bank; but things had changed. This was now a big capital-intensive business. Lack of financial contacts in the great money centers pretty much confined these people to borrowing at relatively high costs from local banks.

As returning soldiers created the need for further building in the community, the country doctor was overwhelmed by events. Unable to achieve access to capital, he would be forced to sell his little company to an entrepreneur who began linking systems together. In the process, the medicine man, the undertaker, and the veterinarian became comparatively rich. (Parenthetically, the dial telephone was, in fact, invented by an undertaker, and the cradle telephone by an independent operator. Many innovations did not originate with AT&T.)

Larger companies were formed that now had assets in the hundreds of millions, headed by people who saw the future in telecommunications. Growth in the suburbs and then the hinterland matched growth in the cities, and owning an independent telephone company was a profitable venture.

When Kyle Rote and Meadows appeared on the scene, the process of consolidation had just begun. After confirmation of Stromberg's interest, and the assurance that there would be someone on the board who understood the business, I committed the $1.5 million, and the Trans Alaska Telephone Company was born.

I had considerable success in start-up companies, and had developed a close relationship with men or organizations of substance. I confidently committed $150,000, and raised the rest of the money from nine interested parties who each sent me a check for $150,000. Among them were Sylvan Coleman and Henry Crown from General Dynamics, Tubby Burnham of Drexel Burnham Lambert, and Ferdie Laval of Dreyfus International Grain. Altogether I made nine calls, and each of the recipients agreed to enter the game.

In those days, telephone utility executives operated an eighty-five-year-old monopoly which they thought would never change. My instinct told me that it was one industry due for some unexpected shocks. We formed a new corporation, called it (rather grandiloquently) Continental Telephone, and I assumed the position of chairman, though no one was under a delusion with respect to my knowledge of the business. Stromberg Carlson provided a Mr. Pritchard as a director who, they assured me, was financially literate and extremely reliable. I had agreed on a reporting system whereby I received weekly reports of a minor nature and monthly analyses showing where the big money was going. I looked for certain key relationships, revenues, and expense streams, and in which direction they were going. I could very rapidly determine whether things were progressing in the right direction, and though I may not have known exactly what was wrong, I could sense whether success or failure was in the cards.

After about three months, I began to sniff the odor of performing seals. In order to head off any opprobrium from my investors, I paid an unannounced visit to Alaska. My first official act in Anchorage was to bail Pritchard out of the local pokey where he had luxuriated the previous night. During his participation in a fight in a local bar he had been relieved of his wallet, which included his identification. In the offices of our vast telephone empire, I realized that something resembling The Great Train Robbery had occurred and had not even been noticed by the toss pot from Stromberg who was protecting our interests from a barstool.

I was sufficiently angered to call the Rockefeller Center office of Jim McLean, then president of Stromberg Carlson, and say, "I want you to send two of your smartest young men to Anchorage to assess the damage. They are to do whatever it takes to rectify our problem." In the meantime, I fired Pritchard and set off for the Racquet Club in Palm Springs to drown my sorrows. In this enterprise, at least, I had discovered the secret of how to strike when the iron is cold.

Stromberg responded splendidly. They sent a chap by the name of Philip Lucier, and a young Australian assistant by the name of Warren Schomaker. It did not take them long to discover that our entrepreneurial Mr. Meadows had laid cable halfway between Kenai and Anchorage with the idea that once that exchange was complete and people were paying for telephone service, we would have a viable enterprise that might properly borrow money to build another exchange, and so on.

He then built a second system halfway to North Pole, Alaska, so now he had spent the money, built half of two telephone exchanges, and achieved the delightful position of having absolutely no income. Phil Lucier arrived in Palm Springs with the news that, had he built the authorized network to Kenai, we would have been creating income and preparing ourselves for growth. As matters stood now, we could be facing a livid population in Kenai, an angry governor and public utilities commission, and shareholders who were ready for revolution.

We solved the problem by having Trans Alaska Telephone engage Continental to run their company for a fee. The damage that had been done in that short period of time was so extensive that it took three years before Contel could finally acquire Trans Alaska. Ultimately, however, all the lines were connected from Kenai to North Pole.

Meadows obviously figured that, since he was dealing with people of financial power and prestige, if the stock took off, he would cash in and take his leave with a million dollars. We did, in fact, buy his stock, but at a very low price because he had not paid much for it to begin with. The last I heard, he was selling motorcycles in Fiji.

Phil Lucier was an exceptionally bright and financially oriented young man with a substantial technical understanding. He had been unsuccessfully beseeching Stromberg to go into the telephone business for three years. "Somebody," he said to me, "is going to do this right; and when they do, they're not going to be able to count the money." I informed Lucier that he was now the president of a yet unformed, unnamed telephone company at a salary of twenty-five thousand dollars a year.

Even though there was (and still is) a frontier mentality in Alaska, it must be said that they have a very socialistic set of business standards. They have great antipathy to outsiders and the cost of doing business is far greater there than in the lower forty-eight.

While we were conducting our deals in Alaska we were unable to find an attorney to help us because the only good one there wanted to work for the interests of the Alaskans. Eventually we had to hire the State's Attorney General for representation. These days, of course, there are more lawyers than caribou. The bureaucracy in that state is worse than in D.C. The only business of any worth there is oil, and the state takes a tithe of every imaginable aspect of the industry: discovery, refining, pipelines. The Alaskans have become potentates on a level with anything in the Middle East.

I now directed myself to reading as much as I could about the telephone industry so that I could shed some light on my new venture. It seemed that it took a long time for people to recognize the potential of the telephone, and in my search I uncovered an extrapolation from a late-nineteenth-century report of the Technical Committee of Western Union, which was then given the opportunity, I am told, to buy the infant American Telephone and Telegraph Company for $100,000:

Report of the Technical Committee
To Determine Market Opportunities for the Telephone

1. The telephone is so named by its inventor, A. G. Bell, who sees for it a vast future as a means of personal communication by voice. He believes that one day they will be installed in every residence and place of business.

2. We note that Bell's profession is that of a voice teacher, and particularly a teacher of the deaf. He appears to have no direct experience with the telephone or any other form of communication, electrical or otherwise. Yet he claims to have discovered an instrument of great practical value in communication, which has been overlooked by thousands of workers who have spent years in this field.

3. Bell's proposal to place his instruments in almost every home and business house (and this is the only way [in] which their potential may be realized) is fantastic in view of the capital costs of installing the endless numbers of wires and cables that

would be demanded. The central exchange alone would represent a huge outlay in real estate and buildings, to say nothing of the electrical equipment.

4. Bell expects that the public will use his instruments without the aid of trained operators. Any telegraph engineer will at once see the fallacy of this plan. The public simply cannot be trusted to handle technical communication equipment. In any home where there are children, to mention only one point, there would inevitably be a high rate of breakage and frivolous use of the instruments. Furthermore, when making a call the subscriber must give the number verbally to the operator and [may] have to deal with persons who may be illiterate, speak with lisps or stammer, have foreign accents and who may be sleepy or intoxicated when making a call.

5. While every telegram consists in itself a written record of what is being communicated, Bell's instrument uses nothing but the voice, which cannot be captured in concrete form, and therefore [there] would be no record of what was said or agreed upon. We leave it to you to judge whether any sensible man would transact his affairs by such a means of communication.

6. Bell expects that the subscribers to this service will pay to have the instruments installed in their premises and will thereby pay for each call made, with a monthly minimum if no calls are made. We feel that it is unlikely that any substantial number of people will agree to such an arrangement in view of the telegraph offices which are now giving efficient round the clock service in every neighborhood and the smallest towns — which charge only for actual messages according to length.

7. In conclusion the committee feels that it must advise against any investment whatever in Bell's scheme. We do not doubt that it will find a few users in special circumstances such as between the bridge of a ship and the engine rooms, but any development of the kind and scale which Bell so fondly imagines is utterly out of the question.

One can excuse a bad guess like this because many of the necessary materials and technologies were probably not available at that time. There is, however, some value to an executive who believes that, within rational limits, if there is a demand for something, creative people will find it. In a comfortable business like a franchised utility, executives could not tolerate being disturbed by a new idea. Before the Second World War, utility executives who dared to suggest straying from established practice might well find themselves in the stocks. Rather than making a decision, these intrepid souls resorted to a pocket veto, which suited me admirably. I had the comfortable feeling that matters of great moment impended.

So it was that, when Phil Lucier arrived at my office in 1961, I had learned a little bit about the possibilities. My banking training suggested that the proper procedure would be to finance a corporation through equity investment, that is, the selling of stock, and after earning money on that investment, to borrow on performance and repeat the process over and over again. I became convinced that the opportunities presented a way of building a mammoth network. Rather than following standard banking procedures, we would take advantage of the Rural Electrification Administration, or REA, which FDR had created in 1935 to encourage the electrification of much of the poor South. At the time, only ten percent of a rural population of thirty million had electricity; by 1950, that would extend to ninety percent. The government would lend money at the rate of two percent, which effectively offered the opportunity of safely borrowing three times as much money as the average businessman could borrow at six percent. We targeted for priority acquisition companies with REA loans, and adopted the policy of saying, "Borrow first, earn money, and finance later," which is exactly the reverse of conventional practice.

I raised another $1.5 million from the same individuals who were already hooked in Trans Alaska Telephone. We could not merge it with the new Continental Telephone Corporation for that would give the appearance of bailing out a bad investment.

Our objective was to create a public corporation that would withstand scrutiny from both the Wall Street community and the SEC.

Phil and Warren Schomaker hired a moderate staff which had experience of utilities. Bob Finch, formerly on the staff of the Illinois Commission, brought us our first candidate, the Millstadt Telephone Company of Millstadt, Illinois, which Phil bought through an exchange of shares in Continental.

We needed a means of contacting potential sellers in an organized way, and my mind went back to the planners at the Prussian war schools. At these gymnasiums, the German military staff had prepared for theoretical wars with an ingenious method of index cards which set forth, in great detail, the military capabilities of any offending country.

It occurred to me that here was an elegant model worthy of emulation. Statistical information on every telephone company was available through the industry representative in Washington, USITA, the United States Independent Telephone Association. This information took the form of balance sheets, profit and loss statements, and a map of the territory in which the company operated. In most cases there was a fairly comprehensive list of equipment and its age.

We moved with such speed that we approved the acquisition of thirty-two small companies at one board meeting. As these companies joined what was rapidly becoming the Continental system, we made a clear plastic overlay of each state which showed our property in that state. With all of this information, we now added a pro forma balance sheet, assuming the acquisition or purchase of a new company, and by simply dropping in the loose-leaf folder the overlay of our property, we could pretty well determine how economically it could operate under one management.

This system worked like magic. If Phil or I received a call from someone saying that they were thinking of selling their telephone company, we would simply flip the pages of our manuals, and we could tell at a glance the position of their property relative to ours. If theirs was an agrarian property, and ours was nearby, we could then immediately have an opinion as to its growth possibilities, as well as the reasonableness of the public utility commission. By looking at the pro forma merge sheets, we could immediately determine the price at which we could make a profitable deal. Assuming that we liked what we saw, we would say, "Yes, we would be quite interested." Since many of us were pilots, in response to a question as to when we could set up a meeting, or whether we would require advance financial information before the first meeting, the proprietor of the telephone company might receive a shock when he heard, "Well, about two o'clock this afternoon?" He would explain that he was in Pennsylvania or New Jersey or Virginia and that it did not seem practical. Our answer was, "If you have a three-thousand-foot airstrip near your exchange, have the Pontiac there at 2:00 P.M., and if you see a tall, bald-headed man get out of a plane, it will be me."

After the usual amenities, a meeting might take this form. The owner would say, "Let me tell you something about our company." Although the probabilities were high that we knew as much as he did, we would listen politely for a reasonable time, and then tour the facility to see the condition of the switch. When we got back to the office, one of us would say, "Mr. Jones, I will give you X number of shares of Continental Telephone for your company. Contel is selling on the American Exchange at such and such a price." We would offer a generous number, and as Mr. Jones's eyes popped, he might say, "Well, this sounds fair. When can I know?" We would then respond, "I just told you." He would ask, "Don't you have to have a meeting?" and we would say, "We've just had one." He would ask,

"What do we do now?" and we would ask if he had an attorney in town, and to get him over there right away. We invariably left with a signed agreement. In the meantime, Mr. Jones, who had also contacted some of our peers, would have received calls asking him to please mail annual reports, balance sheets, and descriptions of his property. Using this method, Continental Telephone was able to buy almost seven hundred telephone companies.

Wall Street watched our amazing growth and noted that we had never bought a property which was a loser. There was one instance, in Henderson, Nevada, where we had obviously overpaid for the system, but we couldn't resist the temptation to test our clout. Henderson was so close to Las Vegas that it was impossible to tell where the one left off and the other began. Central Telephone and Utilities, run by a bellicose gent named Judson Large, was the very conservative company which owned the Las Vegas lines. At the rate the city was expanding, it was obvious to me that they would eventually have to buy the Henderson system. Large coveted this and thought that we had overpaid for it. He called us to express his indignation and to forewarn us of our forthcoming funeral, which he would happily attend. It took eight years of friendly persuasion, but Large eventually capitulated and bought Contel's ownership of Henderson. It was a very profitable deal for us.

Imaginative people like Gil McKay, of McKay-Shields, and Mario Gabelli, who were not rooted in the conservatism of the 1930s business attitude, profited very nicely from their early investment in our company. They may not have been fully aware of the implications of what we were doing, but they certainly knew something innovative and extraordinary was going on.

For the most part, each purchase almost immediately added something to our earnings and efficiency. The secret to our formula was that, unlike other businesses, telephone companies were almost identical. To interconnect with other companies, they had to use equipment compatible with that of every other telephone company, and in general, the means of setting up a network were dictated by AT&T. It was therefore no great deal to look at two companies and determine their worth based upon size, location, and the local economy. Early in the century, in many cities, it was impossible to subscribe to one phone company and have contact with another. This led to great confusion since there were nine phone companies in Chicago alone! When I was a kid, if you were in Philadelphia on the Keystone Sytem, you had to have a different instrument to talk to someone on the Bell System. The last duplicate system was acquired by AT&T in 1945.

There was usually no uniformity of equipment until a 1934 federal law created a legal framework that encouraged interconnection. One of the first things Contel did was to educate the management of a company that we had just bought, because they didn't always know exactly what they needed in terms of equipment. They bought whatever was available at the time for the best price they could find.

Switches were a major headache. Some companies bought Automatic Electric, some bought Stromberg XY equipment, some bought ITT switches. Occasionally the Swedes or Phillips, from Holland, would sell some to this country. Stromberg might have excess inventory of XY switches. They'd sell, say, six hundred switches for a dollar down and a dollar a year for six hundred years. The next time, it might be Automatic Electric who had too big an inventory, so the telco would put that in. We worked together with the telcos as much as possible on what they already had, but it wasn't easy because there would be several different technologies, with the attendant differences in engineering techniques, maintenance, and schedules.

We often bought companies which didn't have a continuous property record, meaning that they really didn't know if they had any open lines. They'd order switches which they didn't need because they simply didn't know how many miles of wire they had to service. They were all amateurs. Contel brought order and unification; we even produced a manual that laid down the guidelines for purchasing, managing, and scheduling. If a manager didn't know what to do in any given circumstance, all he had to do was look in the manual. Management costs dropped dramatically and we could then invest in upgrading the system.

Digital electronic switching is a vital and growing component of our technologies. Contel was the first in the independent industry to use T-1 type digital transmission systems and we were pioneers of the subscriber line carrier. By the middle of the last decade, over half of the entire Continental system was served out of digital electronic offices.

The objective of Contel's programs was to move aggressively into digital electronic switching which would allow for faster, more useful, more economic types of service; in addition it would allow us to provide enhanced grades of service including touch-tone, call forwarding, and much improved times of completion on all local calls. It is an ineluctable fact that institutions must move very actively to increase the traffic-carrying capacity of their telecommunications plants as well as the data-handling capability in the local distribution segment.

There were several significant incidents which marked important steps forward. Owning twenty-one hundred telephones in Millstadt, Illinois, was not the most exciting event in the financial world, but Phil knew of a chap named Jack Maguire who was the principal owner of a small telephone system in Kern County, California. The Kern County Telephone Company had been started by Jack's father, an engineer for Pacific

Telephone. When oil was discovered around Taft, thirty-seven miles from Bakersfield, he successfully applied for the franchise to operate in that area. A single line of telephone poles connected Taft and the Pacific Telephone exchange in Bakersfield.

In no time at all, Kern County telco was a thriving little enterprise, but Jack, who graduated from Stanford with a degree in accounting, had bigger ideas. He envisioned exactly what had been Lucier's dream: the building of a national telephone network for rural and suburban communities, as opposed to AT&T, which was fundamentally for the major cities. GTE at that time pretty much followed the Bell pattern in larger cities where there had been no franchises, with a sprinkling of rural. It was by no means, however, a national system.

I called Jack Maguire, who was considerably less than enthusiastic about the notion of talking with me about a national network, given my credentials, but he said he would send one of his directors to Palm Springs to meet me. The next morning, a rather heavy-set man by the name of Ben Sill appeared at my door and began to talk about everything but telephones. Over a noon-time martini, he asked me if I played golf. I was, by amateur standards, a low handicap golfer, and Mr. Sill did not look athletic enough to enjoy much success against me, so I said, "Ben, I play enough golf to clean your pockets better than the local tailor, so just name the day. In the meantime, let me know if I am welcome to cross the moat of your master's castle."

By way of reply, Ben called Jack Maguire in Bakersfield, and essentially said I was all right and, as an added benefit, looked like ready money on the golf course. The next day, Maguire sent his airplane to fly me to his office in Taft. En route, the plane developed magneto problems and was forced to land near the Women's Prison at Tehachapi, south of Bakersfield, so we had a charming audience while the pilot repaired the engine.

Jack and I hit it off like Damon and Pythias. He was a no-nonsense, first rate accountant, and he knew more about the telephone business than I could learn in a lifetime. Kern County had actually bought two other small systems, at which time they had run out of the financial wherewithal to accomplish the grand scheme that we were up to. He questioned me very closely about my history. He had done some checking, and was cautiously satisfied that I could deliver what I promised, which was money.

At this early point in the game, Jack's system consisted of sixteen thousand telephones. He asked me one question: "If the telephone system in Las Vegas were to come up for sale, could you raise $19 million to buy it?" I said, "If the facts warrant it, I can raise $100 million as easily as I can raise $19 million. Let's get on with the business."

Since it was so early in the game and Maguire was going to provide needed management skills as well as a much larger system, we divided the shares as if he were one of the original entrepreneurs which, in a realistic sense, I suppose he was. Now we had something that began to look like a telephone company. Jack was well known and respected in California. Having been given the assurance of financial backing, he ranged the state, talking to people he knew in the industry, and we began to acquire companies in California. In a few short months, we had built a small system, widely scattered to be sure, but with about sixty thousand telephones. At this moment, I was given the acid test.

Phil Lucier reminded me of my avowed wherewithal to provide large sums of money for the proper opportunities. He announced that he would like us to bid $9 million dollars for the telephone companies owned by the Kirks in Alabama. At this moment, we had about one million in the bank, and a debt-ridden telephone system.

There was no question about the fact that the acquisition of a much larger property, such as those owned by the Kirks, would make us players in the game; if we could get it at an appropriate price, it would be a real winner.

I knew Bob Kerr, one of the principal officers of the Irving Trust Company, and I made the following proposal: "I need a letter of credit for $9 million to acquire these properties. Your security will be one hundred percent of those properties, with a personal written guarantee from me that if we have not paid off half the loan in two years, I will personally buy that half and you may retain the security." He considered this for a moment and said, "Unless you and your people are completely crazy, I think that would be a good deal for the bank. On the other hand, we have a problem. Don Power, who is chairman of GTE, is a director of our bank and chairman of the Utility Committee. General intends to bid for that property, so your loan application will never get past the Utility Committee. However, you are the senior member of a Wall Street house with a splendid credit rating and a good history with the bank. I'll do this as a Wall Street loan." Twenty-four hours later, Phil Lucier left for Birmingham, Alabama, with the $9 million letter of credit clutched in his hand. Our bid was not successful and the property went to General, but nobody ever again questioned my ability to deliver what I had promised.

If you lived in Bakersfield and you wanted to hook in to the AT&T long distance lines to call Chicago, you paid American Telephone ten cents for the privilege. Contel was getting a pittance in what was called a universal settlement, but Jack Maguire was not about to be that easily handled. Jack was interested strictly in toll separation. This was a privilege only the big corporations could afford, because you needed a lot of accountants to keep track of the system. It worked on the premise that every telephone call that left the local exchange went on to someplace else; you measured the usage of the telephone at the point of origin of the call. That percentage of the use associated with long distance was minuscule, but multiply it by a hundred million, and you get Jack's idea.

Now, a determination had to be made when a call was transmitted, of how much your line was used, and how much of the Bell line was used. We had to separate the cost and apply a profit to each component. Mountain States Bell was the first to unilaterally settle this determination on us. To which Jack said, "I don't think so." He had done enormous studies to back up his position, and he said "We believe that our share should be this figure, and therefore we'll thank you for a check in that amount." Mountain Bell were incensed and demanded to see our books. Jack calmly said, "That's great; send your people down. We'll make our books available, and incidentally I'd like to see your books."

Bell knew they were overcharging incredibly on long-distance to subsidize their local telephony. Every time we met with a different Bell unit, we had this same talk. We became the only telephone company whose toll revenues exceeded our local revenues; they proved much greater, relative to our local revenues, than any other telephone company in America. But nobody figured it out for a while. We'd buy a company based on their regular toll settlement and then apply our own formula to lift our revenues.

The telephone business was worthless if we were giving unlimited universal service for one flat monthly fee. The only variable that we could see was the toll revenues. So now, when we deployed capital, we didn't build extensive local networks. We would ultimately be the first company to put in rotary dialing, then touch-tone dialing and automatic dialing. That's why we grew so tremendously. We spent at twice the national average for the installation of toll. It was hair-raising, because we were over-leveraged, but this business was growing by leaps and bounds.

At the end of our first year as Continental, our Annual Report featured a photo from the hit Broadway show *Bye Bye Birdie*. My friend Edward Padula was the musical's producer in 1960, and he permitted us to use the famous shot of a huge gang of kids bidding farewell to their idol Conway Birdie, played by Dick Gautier, as he goes off to join the Army.

A pressing order of business was to carefully examine the structure of the industry and evaluate the competition. It was obvious to me that there was a mutual distrust between AT&T and the independents. No organized effort was made to determine whether they had a communality of interests at any level. AT&T dictated the design of the network, and the independents had no option but to acquiesce.

To break this pattern, I set myself the task of meeting the major figures in the industry. The obvious first choice was the chairman of AT&T, John DeButts. This turned out to be a formidable appointment to make, but I finally hit upon a conduit to the top.

The most powerful man on the floor of the Stock Exchange was John Coleman. The son of a policeman, he had risen to exert more influence on the operations of the New York Stock Exchange than anyone else in history. He was responsible for all of the investments for the Catholic Church in this country, and, because of his imposing presence, few could deny his requests for charitable donations. At John's behest, I had conducted a very successful campaign as chairman of the Cardinal's Committee for the Laity on Wall Street. He, in turn, became cochairman of the Federation of Jewish Charities. John was also a director of New York Telephone, and arranged for me to meet John Scanlon, who was the financial vice-president of AT&T.

Scanlon and I hit it off very well, and in a few short weeks I was lunching with John DeButts, a man with whom I maintained a splendid relationship until after he retired.

It seemed to me that I could deliver a valuable message to DeButts about the necessity for good relations with the rural communities and their systems. I impressed upon him the importance of making common cause with the independents and their friends in Congress: "John, you have to understand that these guys in Yazoo City, Missouri, know their representatives by name. They sit around the cracker barrel with them and swap stories as they eat a pickle." DeButts never really came to terms with that.

American Telephone gave lip service to the notion of disbursement for a while, but they still wanted to dominate all committee meetings. When Contel had first approached the independents they had thrown us out, too; but we stayed friendly with them and eventually even the most rugged of the individualists came around to our way of thinking. Flexibility was a skill that American didn't learn until it was too late.

Some of the traditional phone companies were not very receptive to Contel's aggressive agenda of acquisition. They viewed us as the alien hordes scaling the ramparts of the republic. I received some hilarious telephone calls after the announcement of certain acquisitions. A case in point came from the metropolis of Tom Bean, Texas. Mr. Tom Bean, suzerain of the Tom Bean National Bank, announced that the telephone service was so terrible that he had torn the phone out of the wall and thrown it through the plate glass window at the front of his bank. He went on to promise that if the problem was not solved immediately, he would come looking for us. I called our manager in Texas to find out what the hell was going on in Tom Bean, Texas. He said, "I haven't any idea. We don't own the company. It is owned by General Telephone." I called my friend, Les Warner, chairman of GTE, and advised him to stay out of Texas but to send an armored car to the Tom Bean National Bank and fix the telephone.

When we reached one hundred thousand telephones, or access lines as they are called, in our system, we began to feel like giants, but realized that this was simply one step up the ladder. One day, Jack Maguire alerted me to a company in Apple Valley, California, which did not seem to be owned by anybody, but which did have its own long-distance system running from Bishop, California, to Lake Tahoe on the Nevada state line. Not only would the acquisition of this property increase the size of our system by almost one-third, but it would launch us into the long-distance business. This acquisition would make us second only to General Telephone in California, so Jack urged me to find out where control of this public corporation rested and if it were available.

I discovered that, although there was an Apple Valley common stock trading in the area of 27 a share, control actually rested in the hands of four insurance companies, each one of which had bought Apple Valley convertible preferred stock some years before. The conversion feature was without much appeal since the preferred was convertible at 40 per share into common stock.

When I drew a report on the company, I found that the senior executive of one of these insurance companies, Pacific Mutual, was a very good friend of mine, and another of the directors had been my attorney in the Anza real estate deal. I explained to these two directors that I was interested in purchasing control of the corporation by means of buying their preferred stock, but that I did not want to become involved in an unfriendly tender. Our interest was extremely welcome to those members of the board who had a terrible feeling that their certificates would be buried with them someday, and they asked me if I would prepare a proposal.

Its public price was meaningless. Our best guess was that at fifty dollars the company would be fairly priced; at anything below that, a steal. The portfolio managers of each of the four insurance companies, agreed to sell their preferred stock at forty a share, so I had bought all four blocks, which converted at sixty percent of the equity of the corporation.

I then suggested to the president of the telephone company in California that I could control the corporation by converting the preferred stock, but would rather work out a friendly merger between our two companies. I offered to leave him in charge of his own company and also let him assume the management of several of our properties south and east of Los Angeles. He readily agreed. We were now in the long-distance business.

By a coincidence, two very dear friends of mine, Don Stralem and Tubby Burnham, had started out eight years earlier on the same path upon which we were now embarking. Donald was now a senior partner of Hallgarten & Co., and approximately half of Continental's original investors were common to both our companies. In eight years, however, they had only reached the level of one hundred thousand telephones which we had achieved in a year. Our mutual friend and investor Ferdie Laval urged us to consider a merger.

At the Broad Street Club over lunch one day, Sylvan, Don, Tubby and myself held a meeting. Don opened by saying, "You're on thin ice. You are going at this thing backwards. Get your equity capital in place first. Then borrow against that equity to buy new properties, and when they begin earning money on the borrowed capital, repeat the process." I replied, "Don, the reason you have one hundred thousand telephones in eight years and I have one hundred thousand in one, is that I know there's something special happening today that must be approached in a much more aggressive fashion. I don't want to debate our relative positions, but I have a suggestion to make. Let's meet for lunch one year from today, here at the Broad Street Club, and continue this conversation." One year later, we were almost three times their size and acquired their company, the Independent Telephone Corporation.

After we had completed the acquisition of Independent Telephone, we were a constant topic among companies in the financial district and very soon, with the help of some Wall Street firms and our burgeoning reputation, we acquired a sizable Chicago-based holding company, Telephone Inc., which brought us very close to the half-million mark. They were controlled by a small investment banking firm, but finance was not the long suit of the small telephone companies, and many of them had cheerfully financed equipment by very expensive means. There is no more costly method of financing a company than through a cumulative convertible preferred stock, and many of these outfits were loaded with just such a burden.

The Telephone Inc. acquisition brought us a rash of new opportunities and invitations. Howard Butcher, a Philadelphia banker who, among other things, was chairman of the General Water Works of Philadelphia, and later the major figure in the Pennsylvania Railroad, invited me to buy his company.

Since his company was so large, Howard would have been one-third owner of the joint system, a consummation that interested me not. We fashioned a deal whereby he could only vote ten percent of his stock until it was either sold in a public offering or, with our permission, as part of a future equity offering we would be making to the public. That story had rather a neat ending. Howard was one of the most imaginative of all financiers whom I have met and about two years after he came on our board of directors, asked me if we would object to his issuing a preferred stock on General Water Works which would be convertible into Continental Telephone common stock. It hell out of there and later advised me that he did not want to be eligible for combat pay.

I was eager to get Contel into the satellite business but Western Union had the government contract. In fact, Western Union had the entire satellite world in its grasp and had put up the first instruments under their Westar Systems. The company, however, had some very foggy thinkers; they thought in terms of money orders and telegrams. They only sporadically planned for the future and didn't fully realize their potential. Western Union didn't have the intellectual resources to design the system which would eventually become the backbone of our modern intelligence services.

They also ran afoul of Fairchild Industries, which owned a company called American Satellite Corporation that had the most advanced receivers available. I went to Ed Uhl, chairman of Fairchild Industries, after I learned that Fairchild was choking to death on American Satellite; they had lost at least a hundred million dollars in investment. I said to Ed, "What you need here is a partner with deep pockets. You've charged off your profits on all the losses that you took in putting American Satellite together. I'm prepared to give you twelve million dollars for half of half of your enterprise; however, I want to run it." He almost kissed me on the lips. American Satellite leased three percent of the Westar system which was also in financial trouble. They had placed an order with TRW to build satellites under an advanced payment schedule. I knew that they had a payment due in five weeks of more than fifteen million dollars. I called Bob Flannagan, Westar's chairman, and asked him how he was going to pay it. He didn't know. Now, Contel leased twenty percent of Westar, so I offered to pay him the total term of the contract upfront and discount the dollars forward. In return, I would buy half of Westar and all of its satellites. Frankly, he was glad to get rid of it. So the joint venture of Fairchild and fense Secretary Dick Cheney, National Security Advisor Brent Scowcroft, and Joint Chief of Staff Colin Powell. I was privy to all but Presidential access material, but my brother Albert, a top defense analyst, had even higher clearance; we had to have an understanding that there were certain questions I simply could not ask him. Mr. Bush told me later that the communications system we installed in the Gulf was the finest piece of work he had ever seen.

Charles & Rose, Palm Springs, 1950's

10

DIVERTISSEMENTS

In a lifetime of diverse and unusual enterprises, I have never found a single one that could encompass all of my interests or passions. Even in the sixties, in the first flush of excitement at Contel, when day by day I could revel in the creation of something new, when I could see slowly taking shape a venture that exceeded in scope and complexity all of my previous undertakings, when I would criss-cross the U.S.A. to make an acquisition and find myself in some forgotten town whose name was familiar to me only because some great second baseman had been born there — even in those palmy days, I dreamed of other worlds to conquer, or, at least, to visit and enjoy. I was lucky enough to find them. I became in quick succession (some would say in a fit of absence of mind) the owner of a legendary California watering hole; the proprietor of a wine-producing chateau in Bordeaux; and one of the directors of a foundation to support the Arts.

Before World War Two, Palm Springs was a sleepy little desert town with a population of about eight hundred, located one hundred and five miles over very uncertain roads from Beverly Hills. The center of social life for the weekenders from the motion picture colony was the Racquet Club. In 1938, the club consisted of two tennis courts and a bar which had been designed by Mitch Leisen, director of the Colbert-Barrymore classic *Midnight*. One of the club's proprietors was Charlie Farrell, who had been a great silent-movie star, and had teamed with Janet Gaynor in 1927's *Seventh Heaven*. In the thirties, Charlie and Janet were dubbed "America's favorite lovebirds." The Oscar-winning Miss Gaynor would come to the club even into the late-1940s to attend local affairs for the Rotary Club and the patrons would give an enthusiastic round of applause. She was getting rather matronly by then, and there was something incongruous about the picture as she stood there basking in the adulation, with romantic music playing in the background.

Charlie Farrell, Paul Lukas, and Ralph Bellamy were all tennis enthusiasts and they bought the land in Palm Springs, which was just sand, for $50 an acre. Accommodations were minimal, with only twelve bachelor rooms, each scarcely big enough to contain a bed.

Errol Flynn, Spencer Tracy, Clark Gable, Lana Turner, and William Powell, as well as directors like Mervyn LeRoy and Edmund Goulding, were among the many great names in the movie business lounging around the tennis courts and the bar. Lew Wasserman, currently chairman of MCA, and his wife, Edie, were regulars.

An occasionally appearing face belonged to John Barrymore. The most illustrious Broadway actor of the 1920s was answering the siren call of talking pictures. The walls of the Racquet Club boasted pictures of Farrell and Barrymore nose-to-nose; their profiles bore a remarkable resemblance. Another common trait was their love of the bottle. Barrymore was unquestionably an Olympian imbiber, following in the alcoholic footsteps of his father, the great thespian Maurice Barrymore, who once observed that "staggering is a sign of strength. Weak men are carried home."

It was at the Racquet Club in 1938 that Bob Hope recounted to me the tale of one of the low moments in his life. His real first name was Leslie, but he toured with Fatty Arbuckle in the twenties as Lester T. Hope. He preferred Bob, and was so billed in 1930 when he was playing solo on the vaudeville circuit. His act, booked into towns such as Scranton and Wilkes-Barre, had him posing as a hotel clerk behind a small desk and carrying on conversations with imaginary arrivals. On the first occasion in which he appeared at a slightly better theater, his name was to finally appear in print. He rushed down to the printers, scooped up a copy of the program, and his heart stopped, for there was the billing:

BEN HOPE — WITTY STORIES

He stumbled back to the theater and confronted the unshaven, cigar-chewing manager. Bob accusingly threw the program on the desk and said, "My name is not Ben Hope, it is Bob Hope." The slob shifted his cigar to the other side of his mouth and demanded, "Who else knows?" Since the day he told me that yarn, I have addressed Bob as Ben. By any other name, I certainly preferred Hope to his screen sidekick Bing Crosby. They were both welcome as Palm Springs regulars, but the Groaner was a holy terror when he was drunk.

Stars never felt that they were on display at the Racquet Club, and a tennis match between Gilbert Roland and Errol

Charles, Deloris Hope & Bob Hope, *The Highlander*, 1970's

Charles, Anita Louise & Richard Rodgers The Racquet Club, 1950's

Flynn or Kirk Douglas and Lloyd Bridges was not unusual. No one ever asked for an autograph. Gawkers were politely discouraged. On one occasion, I was sitting at a table in the bar with Clark Gable, Mervyn LeRoy, and William Powell; at a nearby table were Lana Turner and several people from Metro-Goldwyn-Mayer. I went to the bar to pick up a beer and was accosted by two ladies who, judging by their twang, were obviously from the Midwest. They asked me if I could point out some movie stars to them.

I called over to Gable, who was fifteen feet away and said, "Do you see any movie stars here? This lady would like me to point one out." Gable, sporting shades, innocently shook his head and said, "I haven't seen any." Turning to Powell he asked, "Have you, Bill?" Powell admitted that he hadn't, and it transpired that Lana Turner's vision was similarly impaired. The ladies left in disappointment.

Another member of the group was Gregson Bautzer. As handsome as the best of the movie stars, and the most powerful attorney in the film colony, Greg was also a lover of no minor renown. His liaisons included affairs with Joan Crawford, Lana Turner, Dana Wynter, and Ginger Rogers.

I caught my first view of Greg one day while driving along Rodeo Drive, which was then a quiet residential street. He was gazing up at a second-floor window, through which came a torrent of shirts, shoes, and underwear. This parody of Romeo and Juliet's balcony scene was periodically punctuated by Joan Crawford's face screaming at him to never darken her towels again. I met Greg a few nights later and he laughed about it but thought that the audience had been too small, given Crawford's star status and his passionate performance. Joan, by the way, was still married to Franchot Tone at the time.

Over the years, the regulars at the Racquet Club gravitated

toward my private table; attendance was by special invitation only. On any given afternoon you might see Dinah Shore and Barbara Marx (now Sinatra); Rita and David May (he of the department-store clan); Jerry Orbach and his beautiful wife; jet setters Mary Joe and Pat De Cicco; Nancy and Henry Ittleson, chairman of CIT; or Paul and Ruth Zuckerman. Mrs. Zuckerman, as a young girl, was Ruth Taylor, the original Lorelei in the silent screen version of *Gentlemen Prefer Blondes*. Paul, a member of the New York Stock Exchange, was perhaps Humphrey Bogart's best friend, and a wildly funny man. Paul and Ruth are also the parents of comedian and film director Buck Henry. Greg Bautzer and Rose and I, along with a few others, made up the entire complement.

People would rotate between the tennis court and the bar, and we generally had such an amusing time that we often just stayed there and had dinner in our tennis clothes.

One week in the 1950s, Lena Horne was scheduled to appear at the Chi Chi nightclub, and all of the wives decided that we would catch her act over dinner that evening. David May and Henry Ittleson had been playing gin at Bautzer's that afternoon. David, who was an expert card player, protested that he wanted to continue his gin game with Henry, who was a notorious loser at the table. David's wife, Rita, was the stepdaughter of Mervyn LeRoy, and an especially beautiful and self-possessed lady. She snapped, "Dammit, David, you are rich enough not to play gin with Henry!" With a look of wonder in his eye, he retorted, "Honey, nobody is rich enough not to play with him."

In 1968, my friend Donald Stralem and I bought the Racquet Club in order to prevent Ben Silberstein from turning it into another Beverly Hills Hotel. Don was the son of Kassim Stralem, a major figure in the German banking house of Hallgarten and Company, and he eventually became the senior partner in the firm. Don was one of the earliest members of the

Racquet Club, and by the time I met him in 1938 he had been there for almost six years. He was a very fine tennis player, a great looking guy, and a terrific ladies man. When he married his wife, Jean, who was the daughter of Heidelbach Ickleheimer, he bought a home near the club. Don and I eventually became competitors in the telephone industry, but we remained good friends.

When Don and I thought about the good times we had had at the club, we knew we had to save it. We agreed that every dollar we made we would put back into making the club more beautiful and luxurious. We never cuffed a drink or dinner and we always paid dues like every other member. That's exactly how we ran it for the next twelve years, until Don died in 1980.

The club remained the hideaway for the likes of Gene Kelly, William Holden, and Joan Collins. One night, soon after Don's death, someone complained to me that his steak was too well done. I decided right there and then that I did not want to be an innkeeper, so I sold out.

Traveling in Europe, I made many trips to France to visit the best vineyards. It was a very special and graceful world. Through Douglas Dillon, who had been a United States ambassador to France, I met his cousin Seymour Weller, the head of Dillon Read in Paris. Happily, we shared a friendship with Sam Aaron, doyen of one of the great wine purveyors in America.

Weller loved France, so much so that when he became enamored of a charming French lady and married her, he became a citizen of France. All this would be quite unremarkable were it not for the timing: Seymour took out his citizenship in August of 1939, just before the German invasion of Poland that started World War II.

In the early thirties, on behalf of the Dillons, Weller had engineered the purchase of one of the great premier *grand cru* châteaux, Haut-Brion. Everything came to a halt during the war, when Haut-Brion became a rest home for Luftwaffe officers. In order to protect the great antiques and Persian rugs in the châteaux from the Nazis, Weller cleverly hid them in the shanties of the people who toiled in the vineyards. No self-respecting German officer would imagine that these shacks sheltered treasures. Moreover, Seymour became active in the French underground and had some hair-raising experiences with British air drops and dodging the Gestapo. At war's end, the Germans left, and the furniture was returned to the château.

Through Sam Aaron, Seymour contacted me from Paris to announce that I should forsake all else, that opportunity was knocking insistently at my door. This great chance was nothing less than the availability of one of the grand châteaux in the Bordeaux area. He explained that it was about one hundred and thirty-six acres and that the house was a national treasure. Above all, they produced a *cru classé* wine which, in his view, could be improved to reclaim its *grand cru* status: Seymour assured me that it was just the thing for my friend Howard Sloan and me. It could have been fitted by my tailor. He further claimed that this was the first château of this caliber offered for sale in more than twenty-five years.

I translated this for him. "Seymour, if I understand you correctly, you are looking for somebody who is rich enough and stupid enough to buy a château in France." He answered that I unfairly misjudged him and that I should not scoff, for this was a rare favor reserved for a good friend. He assured me this could be accepted as Holy Writ; I would fall in love with the place.

I believed that Seymour was the soul of honor and could be trusted. I admit freely that in this case, however, I doubted whether his testimony could survive a slashing cross-examination, but my curiosity was aroused. And so it was that the next day, I was en route to Paris with Howard to meet Seymour and journey thence to the commune of Cadaujac, in the famous Graves area, about eleven kilometers from Bordeaux. One look at this magnificent house, and all was lost. We were sinking like the Titanic. Howard, being cut of the same cloth as I, first asked for immunity and pleaded that he was only there to see that I got home safely. I fixed him with an unblinking stare and said: "Quit it. Are you in?" Drawing on his unparalleled command of English, he said: "Yes."

We engaged a Harvard-educated French attorney by the name of François Monahan, who represented Dillon, General Motors, and other great American corporations. Now he had a less distinguished new client. From his formidable invoices, Howard and I decided that he had us confused with General Motors, but the dice were thrown, and the negotiations were soon concluded.

If nothing else, the name François Monahan was enough to engage our attention. He was a product of a marriage between a French lady and an Irish-American. He entertained us lavishly and served excellent wines in his beautiful home in Paris. A limousine awaited us at the Ritz hotel and delivered us to Monahans' apartment. We noted that he was a generous host. We did think it a bit much that a month or so later we were billed for the cost of the dinner, for however splendid the ambiance in the Monahans apartment, it was not equivalent to Taillevent. We became quite careful with our new representative, and only asked his opinion of the weather after careful thought. French lawyers, after all, are much like their American counterparts.

It became apparent early on in discussions that one of the

things that makes excellent sense if you are going to make wine is that you'd better have someone who knows how to do it; in France, this presents quite a problem. We did not inherit a manager, or a *gérant* or *régisseur*, to effectively supervise the making of the wine and determine the mix of grapes; the magician who selects that particular moment in time signals exactly when the grape should be harvested. Make no mistake, the ability to select the right date has an enormous impact on the quality of the wine, and a heavy rain during the *vendange* or harvest can produce grape juice instead of wine. Once again, Seymour made an extraordinary arrangement for us by providing a *gérant* by the name of Jean Delmas, son of the greatest wine maker in France, and producer of the wine at Château Haut-Brion, which was the property of the Dillon family. It was almost inconceivable in France that one *vigneron* would share his greatest treasure with another. Chalk up one for the Dillons.

We were very soon busily engaged in furnishing the interior of the château with the assistance of Madame Anne Delmas, a provincial French lady, simple but lovely. Meanwhile, Americans that we were, we began construction of a good-sized exterior swimming pool and pool house. This turned out to be a Herculean feat, since the French contractor saw nothing objectionable in building a pool that leaked. We found that somewhat inconvenient. Before the pool would hold water properly, it was rebuilt three times, but it was worth it. The pool lay behind the château, abutting a fifty-acre park in which we could walk in the morning and pick berries for breakfast. Finally, counseled by Billy Talbert, the former Wimbledon tennis champion, captain of the American Davis Cup team, we built a beautiful tennis court. Billy was a great wine buff himself.

Along with the château, we purchased an inventory of six hundred thousand bottles of Château Bouscaut, with vintages going back to the 1920s. The purchase of that inventory was an afterthought and a confirmation about how the Fates take care of dumb, well-meaning people. In our interest in buying the castle and its vineyards, we ignored the most rudimentary rules of agronomy: we only thought of that moment when we would be delivering this new heady wine of ours; we cleverly assumed that the day after we became the châtelaines, we would wave some kind of a magic wand and produce wine directly from the grapes. What is more, it would be delivered already bottled, without going through the formalities involved in fermentation and the mixing of different blends that would distinguish one wine from another. We forgot the elementary fact that good wine is not bottled until two years after it has finished fermenting. In the intervening time there is a need to carefully remove impurities, scrupulously select the proper color during the pressing, and perform all of the other functions that distinguish wine from Pepsi-Cola. So it was that we had bought a château and were busy closing the deal knowing we would probably be out of business for three or four years.

In the final minutes before signing, we were rescued by the owner of Château Bouscaut, who proved to be even more naive than we. After we had gone through the legal processes, he casually observed that he was certain that Howard and I would not object to his continuing to store the six hundred thousand bottles of wine currently resting in the château until he could dispose of them. In an assumed state of shock, Howard and I exchanged glances and of one voice, said: "Oh, Mr. Place, we really did not buy the château to use it as a warehouse. We are certain that you will be able to arrange storage in some warehouse in Bordeaux." Since this was a very unlikely prospect, and would involve moving and storage with all their attendant dangers, the seller was aghast. We solved our mutual problem by agreeing to buy the entire inventory at a few francs a bottle, without regard to vintage. We were now in a position to put our own label on wine grown in the twenties and, with a straight face, sell it to all the wine lovers in the world. We were now ready for business *and* pleasure.

At this juncture, Seymour took me aside and said, "I don't want you to misunderstand this, but I am going to give you some advice. You're going to meet most of the wine growers in the Bordeaux area, you'll be invited to functions given by the American Consul, Dixon Boggs. No matter how friendly the other guests seem, in no circumstances should you initiate a move to invite them to Bouscaut for luncheon or dinner. The French are very strange about this and abhor pushy Americans. I know you well enough, and I'm sure you will be made welcome in good time. When that moment comes, they will invite you first, after which you can reciprocate; I guarantee that you'll have warm friendships with the community of *vignerons*."

For the most part the grand châteaux were owned by the élite. The Rothschilds own Lafite Rothschild and Mouton Rothschild. Château Latour was owned by Lazard Brothers in London, and other châteaux were owned by counts. Seymour was right; we carefully avoided making waves and soon had become part of a group of the most charming and attractive people, whose friendships still endure.

Usually, when we arrived at our ancestral castle, Rose might call Dixon Boggs (his wife's name was Reine, which means "queen" in French) and say, "Boggsy baby, close the Consulate. You and Queenie get over here for tennis and champagne this afternoon." We would invite Daniel Lawton of the Cruse family, Alain and Brigitte Mihaille, the proprietors of Pichon Longeville and Château Palmer, and several others. It was a grand way to live.

Since our objective was not influenced by the rank odor of profit, we determined not to have traffic with any inferior wine. We agreed never to bottle anything but a good wine. But in

1968, the first year in which we harvested, the rains came during the *vendange* and we produced about eighteen thousand cases of borscht which were sold on the Bordeaux market at five francs a bottle. This caused me to remember some advice my mother had given many years before: "Son, never buy anything that eats." Forewarned by this sage advice, I had no interest in race horses or such, but now we had about eighty people who cared for the property and the vines, which is really a twelve-month process. We provided housing for families which had been attached to the château for as long as a hundred years. Some of them had never seen Paris, which was only three hundred miles away. They ate. We were saved only by our inventory.

Howard and I invited friends from California, Seattle, and New York to take a rooting interest in Bouscaut, for we planned to sell in the U.S. market. We all knew the great American restaurateurs and we counted on getting on their wine lists nationwide.

The subtle cachet of being a *vigneron* was validated a few years later. I was in Tokyo, entertaining the chairmen of Nippon Electric and Nomura Securities at dinner, when I saw Bouscaut on the wine card at the Okura hotel. With false innocence I ordered it. On seeing the label with the legend "Domaine Wohlstetter, Sloan," the inscrutable Orientals raised their eyebrows and nodded their heads in respect.

At first, we had not considered the social implications in the purchase of Château Bouscaut. There was a considerable amount of publicity in the Bordeaux and Paris newspapers, and it was picked up in the United States. Since the people involved generally patronized the finer eating places and traveled regularly, we were followed by a growing interest on the part of our friends. Invariably, one would say: "Why didn't you tell me you were going to do this? I would have loved to be part of it." All of this was very flattering, but I had long ago learned that between a profession of deep interest and the investment of a dollar there is frequently a chasm which cannot be brooked. On the other hand, we were warmly greeted in restaurants by the sommelier and the proprietor, and we saw friendly sommeliers wink at us very ostentiously and recommend our wine to a nearby patron. After the gesture of approval on the quality of the wine, which was almost automatic in any event, I would be introduced to the patron as the proprietor of the château that grew that wonderful wine. This would be done with a flourish and we took on a new and more prominent social stature. It was really great, because during the course of dinner at gourmet restaurants, the sommelier would frequently pass our table and, out of the corner of his mouth, give us a tally on the number of bottles sold that evening.

I had suddenly become a wine expert and was invited to lecture on French wines at the Bordeaux society in Beverly Hills, whose ranks included Walter Pidgeon, Burgess Meredith, and some of the great movie stars. I was elected a *Chevalier du Tastevin*, and then a *Commandeur of the Commanderie de Bordeaux*, finally achieving the eminence of *Grand Commandeur*. I have a picture of me in a long velvet coat with a white ermine collar, a glass of Bordeaux wine in my hand, standing before members of the French Academy of wine during a test of my knowledge prior to induction in Bordeaux. (I am glad that my comments on the wine were not recorded.) I displayed my *vingeron's* education before groups in New York, Chicago and at telephone conventions. If I was introduced as a speaker, my ownership of Château Bouscaut identified me as someone outside of the ordinary pattern in the business. From 1968 to 1980 I was a major owner of the Racquet Club and Château Bouscaut, two of the most glamorous and interesting places I had ever visited.

It was surely the right time and the right place, because although neither of these spas was bought with a profit motive, they each paid huge dividends in pleasure and, less importantly, were sold at substantial profits. A sensible person might ask: "Why in the hell would you sell Château Bouscaut?" François Mitterrand was elected in France with loud promises of nationalizing everything in sight. I had visions of M. Mitterrand nationalizing the farms, including Bouscaut. He did, in fact, start out on a tack of nationalizing industries and nearly drove France into bankruptcy and despair. How was I to know he would reverse himself?

Howard and I discussed the matter and, since the franc was at that time four to the dollar, as wily economists we assumed that within a year it would fall out of bed. And so it did. About a year after we sold our lovely house in France, the franc was nine to the dollar. With some satisfaction, I announced to my wife that the difference between four francs and nine francs to the dollar equated to more than a million dollars. Unimpressed, she politely said: "I see. What did you do with the money? Is it in a bank? Have you bought some beautiful colored stock certificates? Tell me, have you enriched our lives any? How do we replace Bouscaut?" It only took three seconds to realize that she was right, and we should never have associated that wonderful vineyard with business.

In February 1966, Billy Rose paid the price for being a chain smoker. After a series of heart operations, he died of lobar pneumonia in a nursing home in the West Indies. He was sixty-six years old.

I would be disingenuous if I said that I felt a great sense of loss or that his passing left a hole in my life. Billy was, to be sure, a good friend and a source of many memorable amusements, but in the matters that really interested me, from a long-term perspective, he did not exert a lasting influence.

He left a fortune of about $38 million, which would be the equivalent of several times that amount today. He recognized that he had never been able to give money during his life, and was uncertain about how it should be disbursed in the future. Aside from some small bequests to his sisters and to Joyce, Billy left the entire fortune to the Billy Rose Foundation, and named a distinguished lawyer, James R. Cherry; a Broadway producer, Arthur Cantor; his personal lawyer, Morris Shilensky; and myself as the directors of the foundation.

He named me chairman, a position that has rotated among the members of the foundation ever since. He essentially left us no instructions, stating that we were selected because of our associations with philanthropic giving, and that we knew him well enough to judge what could best express his love of the country. It has been a privilege for us to make grants of a memorable nature to the visual and performing arts, to libraries, to medical centers, and, very particularly, to young theater and opera groups.

One of our grants, for example, went to John Houseman: he wanted to start a repertory company with the graduates of his theater program at Juillard. I have the great pleasure of knowing that his production of Chekhov's *The Three Sisters* which we funded featured the Broadway debuts of both Kevin Kline (Vershinin) and Patty Lupone (Irina). I think Billy would be pleased.

Some of the choices posed to us were less clear-cut. I was approached by one of my employees at IMC Magnetics, a man by the name of Jack Feldman. Jack had an eighteen year-old son who played the cello and had been invited to play with the Boston Symphony Orchestra. Unfortunately he had no instrument, so Mr. Feldman asked me if the Rose Foundation could help. I pondered for a moment and then said, "The government would frown on such a deal because it is not a deductible expense. However, if I make a gift of a cello to Boston University, they may then lend it out to deserving youngsters such as your son." That is precisely what I did, and the young man went on to success as a musician and conductor. Three years later, Jack approached me again. "Mr. Wohlstetter, I have another son who is a pianist." I cut him off. "Sorry, Mr. Feldman. No pianos!"

Each of these *divertissements* offered its own rewarding fantasy. At the Racquet Club, I could feel like Bogie in *Casablanca*; at the Chateau, I was living in a Lubitsch movie; and in the deliberations of the Rose foundation, I could imagine myself a supporting player in a backstage musical, racking his brain to find a way for the show to somehow go on.

Meanwhile, my daily life at Contel was carrying me literally into a whole new world.

Charles & Adnan Khashoggi, agent of Saudi Arabia's Royal Family,
on Khashoggi's yacht, *The Nabila* circa 1980

11

GOING INTERNATIONAL

B_y the mid-seventies, Continental Telephone was a world-wide corporation. Our affairs were carried on in forty states, and we had offices in Cairo, London, Madrid, Rome, and Riyadh. When the Iran-Iraq war broke out, we were finishing the installation of the infrastructure for the telephone system in Teheran. We had designed the Egyptian telephone system and were doing work in Saudi Arabia, with joint ventures in many other places. Contel had arrived.

Contel's involvement in Saudi Arabia began with an unexpected call from a famous figure. I was in Palm Springs when Mr. Adnan Khashoggi telephoned from Nairobi with the announcement that he was going to make me a very rich man. This sounded extraordinarily generous of him, so I replied that, although I was not a rich man by his standards, my wife and I had very modest tastes and were quite comfortable as we were. He clucked his tongue and said, "I don't think you understand me. I do not propose to make you rich like an American; I am going to make you rich like an Arab." That was an interesting enough observation to catch my attention. He spun a web for me which would have attracted all the flies in the universe, and ended by saying that he would meet me at my convenience any place in the world.

We arranged to meet in London the following week, but when I arrived with my attorney there was a message from Mr. Khashoggi that he was on his yacht in Venice. If I was agreeable, he would have his private plane fly me thence. Every middle-class American boy should be given this kind of treatment at least once in a lifetime, so the following morning, my attorney and I embarked as the sole passengers on a Boeing 727. I admired the gold fixtures in the cabins and was particularly astonished to see that among the conveniences in the master suite was a shower.

It seemed quite unlikely that I would ever be afforded such an opportunity again, so, although the flight to Venice from London lasts only a couple of hours, I decided to sample this airborne luxury. I advised the steward to tell the pilots that I did not really care whether they circled the Adriatic until I finished my shower, I would not be denied this pleasure. I subsequently found out from an officer of Boeing that the cost of this shower had been something like liquid gold.

We were met at the airport by a contingent of people from Triad, Khashoggi's holding company. The group was headed by a Mr. Shaheen, a Lebanese American from Pittsburgh, my first introduction to the kind of people with whom Khashoggi had surrounded himself. In the ensuing months, I was to meet people who had left the quiet safety of Boston or New York banks, and even American universities, to embark on imaginative financial adventures with Khashoggi. His staff was American, young, and bright.

Adnan was the son of King Khalid's personal physician. There were so many princes that Khalil, instead of giving them spending money, would permit them to obtain business contracts for, say, building the roads or expanding the construction industry. The prince with responsibility for telecommunications was King Faisal's son Mohammed, who is now the king.

It was through his familiarity with the system that Adnan had built up his contacts and business savvy, but he also saw that most foreign businessmen who sold to his country did not have the Saudi interests at heart. Khashoggi had a very American point of view and he opened up many channels of communication which had hitherto remained inaccessible. He has the capability of taking vast, widely-diverse problems and bringing them together with a new focus that ties them ineluctably together.

Upon arrival at the Royal Danieli Hotel, we were given some rubber-soled shoes and taken to the beach. As we left the dock, we could see what appeared to be the Queen Mary riding at anchor. We boarded one of the great luxury yachts in the world. We planted ourselves on the aft deck, and in short order the man himself put in an appearance. Adnan proved to be a short, rather pleasant man of generous girth for his height. He was very affable, and we had a general discussion prior to lunch.

The attacks against Khashoggi have been made by people who just read the press and have no personal experience of him. One thing that I've never really heard emphasized is the reason he had so much influence in the Arab world in the first place. When Saudi Arabia began to buy American or French or German products, everybody sold them second-rate stuff; they had continuing problems on every contract and were deliberately overcharged. You can't think of an environment in which they didn't suffer. Along came Khashoggi, who was a new kind of entrepreneur, with fine contacts in the western world and the guts to pick up the telephone and call anybody. He became the first businessman who always delivered to Saudi Arabia exactly what he said he would, at the price he had quoted, within a reasonable amount of time. For instance, he was personally responsible for bringing in Lockheed to run the Saudi air bases, and Lockheed did a terrific job.

Khashoggi's reputation for legitimacy and dependability spread rapidly throughout the Arab world. When I had my first private meeting with Anwar Sadat he said, "Mr. Wohlstetter, not only is Adnan Khashoggi my friend, he is a friend of Egypt's. When I needed many millions of dollars, Khashoggi arranged a loan for me. I am not going to forget that. He wants to be a partner in our telecommunication enterprise; he will put up money, with the other entrepreneurs, just to ensure that the assembly plant in Cairo will be run along the principles of an American business. But he is an equal, not a commissioned salesman. We have a Socialist country here. If I said I paid him a fee, that would be the end of me and the end of everything. This is the best thing that I can do to thank him."

I had been advised by my office that Khashoggi's Triad office in London had asked to forward an extremely full résumé of my life's activities. Also to be included were those things that I admired most or those activities that pleased me most. One of the surprises for our Saudi host was the fact that I was one of the principal owners of that wonderful châteaux near Bordeaux which produced Château Bouscaut. When we sat down to lunch, Adnan apologized to me for not having had the time to send to Bordeaux for some of my own wine, but said he was serving a 1945 Château Haut-Brion, which he flatteringly labeled a first cousin.

During the meal, Khashoggi finally outlined his grand scheme. Saudi Arabia needed a telecommunications system of enormous proportions, but no single company had all the necessary elements to provide it. Khashoggi properly broke the plan down into its component parts: switching could be done by Phillips of Holland, infrastructure by Holsten of Germany, and cabling by Serti of Italy. All that was missing was a central intelligence company to act as a management, maintenance and service organization. Contel's procedures were designed for just such a scheme.

It was about this time, in the late seventies, that the Carter Administration passed an idiocy in Congress called the Foreign Corrupt Practices Act, which effectively removed American business from many valuable markets. Sweden didn't care about it; France didn't; Holland didn't. But our businessmen had to go through the most protracted convolutions to obtain permission to trade with the Middle East. As a result, Contel could not be a prime contractor for Khashoggi's plan, but I offered to put together the package for the other components. In that way, the contract could be evenly divided. Phillips balked at my idea, however, and brought in Bell Canada, who walked in, took over, and took advantage of our work.

In the United States I would have sued them, but the contract stipulated that all legalities were to be handled in the Saudi courts. The Saudi government warned me that, because of the differences in Moslem law, not only would I not win my case in court; I would also lose any chance of future contracts in the Arab world.

My association with Khashoggi led to several private and fascinating meetings with President Sadat of Egypt, who was truly an interesting man, quite informal, with a great sense of humor. When the Camp David accords were signed in the United States, Mustapha Khalil, the Egyptian prime minister, called me in and said, "Charles, you will be invited to a dinner at the White House on Thursday night. Do not accept. This will be a dinner for the people who either gave or raised money for President Carter. President Sadat is giving a small dinner party the following night at the Egyptian Embassy for the people in the United States for whom he feels the greatest kinship." And so it was that on the night following the dinner for fifteen hundred at the White House, I attended a dinner for eight which included Cyrus Vance; Bob Strauss, the U.S. trade negotiator; and John Swearingen, chairman of Standard Oil of Indiana. It was a better party.

Sadat came back to the United States in 1978 to take part in the dedication of the Temple of Dendur exhibition at the Metropolitan Museum. Admission was by invitation only but the walls were bulging. Sadat stood before the entrance to the temple, which was raised above the museum floor by perhaps six feet. I wended my way through the crowd toward President Sadat, clutching my wife's arm as I dragged her with me. I wanted to introduce Rose to him, in which way I hoped to show her what a great marriage she had made. When I was perhaps fifteen feet short of the stairway leading to the front of the temple, and there were still more than fifty people in front of us, the President spotted me and called out, "Mr. Wohlstetter, where are my telephones?" Immediately before his retirement, John DeButts and I, together with incoming AT&T chairman Charlie Brown, had gone over to Egypt to hammer out the details of a three-way enterprise for Sadat. AT&T was to handle transmission, GTE the switching (through their Automatic Electric division), and Contel would take care of training and maintenance. Unfortunately, with the great help of our President and our State Department, the contract had been lost to Siemens of Austria and to the French.

Before I had gone over to make the presentation to Sadat I contacted a teacher I knew in Washington who had been at the American University in Beirut and had lived in Cairo for many years. I said to him, "I want to know something about the mood of the Egyptians, their environment. Tell me what the most acceptable tone is to speak to them." I also wanted to learn something of Egyptian history, so I listened to him and asked questions, and read a couple of books before I sat down to write my speech.

I delivered an impassioned talk about how the confluence of the Blue and White Niles had come together to form this great nation, and related it to the new co-operative enterprise we were now embarked upon. My effort was rewarded by deafening applause and the congratulatory handshakes of what seemed to be the entire Egyptian government.

In the receiving line was a gigantic black man who looked like basketball star Patrick Ewing. He pumped my hand and rumbled, "You have caught the soul of Egypt better than anyone. You must come and see me tomorrow; I must talk to you." He handed me his card on which were printed the words Arab League. I thanked him for his comments, but as I pocketed the card I knew that if I ever went to his office, I would never get out of there again.

Anwar Sadat, contrary to public perception, was not a big fan of Jimmy Carter, a fact he expressed to me privately in very blunt language. The only reason he tolerated Carter at all was because of how he made out in the Camp David accords; Sadat obtained by that agreement land and oil fields that years of war had denied him. Israel, on the other hand, was left with practically nothing from the deal. Carter himself was not against Menachem Begin and Israel, but the prevalent mood in his administration was.

The general mismanagement of Middle Eastern affairs was magnified by the fiasco in Iran. The Shah, for all his arrogance, was pro-Western and much more agreeable to deal with than Khomeini. Though Pahlevi was a very sick man by the time he was deposed, we should still have recognized that, without our support, his rule was in jeopardy. By international law, the exiled Khomeini was not permitted to campaign for reinstatement in his country, and yet the French turned a blind eye to all of his machinations. The least we could have done was protest to the French government, even though, because of the economic promises that Khomeini made, it is unlikely they would have listened.

I was not personal friends with the Shah, but I did know people who knew him and I did have dinner with him once in Paris. He was a very engaging man, a great sportsman fond of fast cars, and a pilot who loved fast airplanes.

One of my partners in Iran, Bahman Batmanghelidj, was a very hard-working individual who could get things done. Bahman's brother, Hooshang, was the Iranian Ambassador to Turkey. The two of them provided me with one of those instances when I was able to laugh at my brother Albert a little bit.

Albert was enormously involved in affairs in the Middle East and was making a trip to Iran and thence to Turkey. I had nearly two thousand people working for me in Iran and I had a very large office there. I knew from experience that, in that part of the world, small nuisances can become incredible catastrophes. Before he left I told Albert, "I ought to give you the telephone number of our office and I will write the head of our operations there that you're coming. That way he can arrange for hotel reservations and for someone to meet you at the airport. That will help you get through customs and ensure that the Arab League don't get their hooks in you." Albert said, "The American Ambassador, William Sullivan, is a good friend of mine. He's making all the arrangements for me. Your involvement might cause an embarrassment." I could see his point, but I did prevail upon him to take the telephone number of my office, just in case.

Albert and Roberta arrived in Teheran and found there was no one from the American Embassy to meet them. But there was Bahman Batmanghelidj waiting with a limousine parked on the tarmac, next to the airplane. And while they settled in the limo, their baggage was checked through customs, and later followed them to the Hilton Hotel in the foothills of the Alborz Mountains. The embassy had failed to make the reservation, but somehow the rooms were miraculously made available. When I spoke to Albert he said, "You have the most efficient and friendly people I've ever seen in this part of the world. They are truly wonderful." I bit back the urge to gloat and graciously said, "Thank you, Albert."

He proceeded to tell me that in three days' time he had an appointment with the Iranian Ambassador to Turkey in Ankara. I told Albert that he should take Bahman Batmanghelidj to lunch to thank him for his assistance. Because he and Roberta had every minute taken up he was a little grudging, but he agreed to my suggestion. Mr. Batmanghelidj never came into Teheran, so he invited Albert and Roberta to his home in the suburbs. Albert's eyes rolled in anguish at this prospect, but when they arrived he discovered that he and Bahman took to one another wonderfully. They spent over three hours in conversation.

Bahman explained that a dinner party was to be given the next night and among the dignitaries in attendance would be the Shah. He arranged for Albert and Roberta to attend. It was indeed a glittering affair, overflowing with caviar and champagne and worldly talk. When Hooshang met Albert and Roberta, he told them, "When you come to Ankara, you must stay at the embassy," which they did.

A couple of months after Khomeini came to power I received a telephone call from Albert, who was worried about Hooshang's whereabouts and wanted me to find him and to assist him if necessary. I did find Hooshang, in Princeton, where his two daughters were attending the university. I told him about my conversations with Albert and Bahman, asked him about his plans and offered to help in any way I could. He very much appreciated the personal concern and my efforts to locate him. He stated that he was not at all sure about his future plans, but that he intended to stay in this country for a while with his wife and daughters. I found out that he was having difficulty in getting the local banks to give him a mortgage loan. I invited him to New York to lunch and arranged his mortgage and guaranteed him.

After Hooshang settled permanently in the United States, we became good friends. We heard that his wife's father, who had been a Senator and a general in the army, had been arrested and executed. The daughters went to Stanford and Harvard, where they were a glowing success. When his daughter Nazee graduated, Hooshang asked if I could help find the right job for her. I sent her to Drexel Burnham, and Tubby Burnham subsequently called to thank me: "This is the brightest kid we ever hired," he said, and she did indeed go on to a great career. The other daughter, Sharmin, is equally brilliant and successful. So it turned out that Albert discovered that the inner bureaucracy in some ways has more power and expediency than the official one.

Like many people at the time, I was aware of the power vacuum that was developing in Iran. I personally visited President Carter in 1978 and urged him to support the Shah on the premise that the priest is preferable to the witch doctor. I felt very strongly that we would be better off dealing with Pahlevi's autocracy than with the militancy of the fundamentalists. His response was typically condescending. He said, "Mr. Wohlstetter, you go on installing the best telephone systems in the world; let the U.S. government take care of foreign policy."

I had been exposed to what passes for American diplomacy in foreign countries before, since Contel owned most of the telephone companies in the Caribbean, and we received the same kind of help from our embassies in these countries as the Kenyan farmers received from the Mau-Mau. Foreign service personnel, including ambassadors, sometimes act as if American businessmen are their sworn enemies.

I had negotiated a four-year contract with the Iranian ministry of Post and Telephones. This was for 500,000 telephone lines sorely needed in Tehran, a city of five million people. Shortly after we started work, rioting broke out in Tehran, then in other parts of the country, and a major curfew was imposed. Bahman Batmanghelidj was very close friends with General Ovayssi, Chief of the Armed Forces, and a General Rahimi, and he was able to obtain permission for us to work during curfew. From dusk to dawn, we had the city to ourselves, putting in telephone lines, digging up the streets, and putting in a major conduit system with phone lines having to traverse water lines, electrical lines, and all the other infrastructure involved. Some 1500 people worked through the night with no interference whatsoever, apart from the occasional military vehicle going by. Bahman's operation was very efficient, and we were able to do the work well within budget, and substantially ahead of schedule. I have to say we were proud to have the "Bahman" brothers as our partners in Iran.

When the Shah's government collapsed and Khomeini came to power, Bahman and his brother Mohammad were successful in convincing the new government that Tehran, which needed at least two million more phone lines, could not afford to discontinue the work. This time with revolutionary guards enforcing he curfew, we continued installing the telephone system. The work went on for at least six months after Ross Perot's little adventure. When it became obvious that the situation was not going to improve, but would result very shortly in the imprisonment of our people, we arranged, with Bahman's help, to get our American workers as far as Turkey, where I had a plane waiting to bring them home. Our exodus was not as well publicized as Perot's but certainly was as efficient. And I didn't run for President.

Clockwise from top: Arnold Palmer & Charles, circa 1970,
Jerry Lewis, unidentified & Charles, circa 1950, Charles & Gary Player,
South Africa, 1976, Charles & Tom Watson, circa, 1980

12

EPILOGUE:
THE RIGHT TIME,
THE RIGHT PLACE

∽

Today, as I have every day for the past decade, I sit at a large walnut desk in my office on the 24th floor of 375 Park Avenue. Before me, all around me, are the small objects and mementos that evoke the events and stages of my life. A penholder with bronze figures of a bull and a bear (from my days on Wall Street) sits next to a desktop coffer of dark wood inlaid with ivory (a present from Anwar Sadat). My wife and three children stare out from a framed photo at the model of a TDRSS communications satellite launched by CONTEL (which seems to orbit a brass Tiffany clock, a gift of Salomon Brothers, commemorating a deal with McCaw Cellular). In another framed photo, Tom Watson and I wander down a fairway seeking nirvana on the golf course.

To the right of me, an antique English bookcase houses an impressive selection of world literature. Pepys's *Diary*, the poetry of Dryden and Byron, the prose of Montaigne and Cicero stand beside minor novelists like Ouida or Octave Mirbeau. None of these attests to my literary taste or lack of it: only to the eye of the decorator who bought the gilt-edged morocco-bound volumes by the boxload from Argosy Books. Still, if I'm not on the phone tossing around words like gigabits and megahertz or evaluating a deal someone has brought in, I will occasionally wander over and browse like a stranger in a bookstore. One day, I vow, when I have less to do, I will read them cover to cover.

I bear the imposing title "Vice-Chairman of GTE." Before that, I was "Chairman of the Board of CONTEL." Tomorrow, I will be "Retired." Titles change but, for me, the scene remains the same: this room, this desk, this comfortable black leather armchair. As I sit and look out the window at Park Avenue, at the glass box of Lever House or the Florentine Renaissance palazzo facade of the Racquet and Tennis Club, I sometimes wonder how exactly I came to be sitting in this chair and not another.

It is always tempting to ascribe one's own success to sheer determination, brains, a capacity for hard work or some other virtue one possesses in abundance, and to discreetly ignore the necessary element of luck which provides us with the opportunities for those virtues to prevail. So much depends on being in the right place at the right time. True, one must have the ability to recognize such opportunities and the skill and energy to take advantage of them, but I have seen many talented and hard-working people fail. There is, finally, an element of mystery. Without pretending to understand it, I can only be grateful for the good fortune I've had.

Still, now that I've reached the age at which one spends

more time reflecting on the past than anticipating the future, the mystery of my presence in this particular chair teases me. How did I end up here rather than in, say, the defense industry, entertainment, real estate, or any of the other areas I've labored in? If I trace my path from playing stickball on Fort Washington Avenue through Broadway, Wall Street, Hollywood, Bordeaux, and the Middle East, will I see along the way a series of roads not taken or just the necessary links in a destiny that leads only here? Do all my diverse projects have anything in common or are they simply, to borrow Shakespeare's famous conceit, among the many parts that one man in his time was called to play?

A young man is thrown into a world in which everyone around him seems to know more, to have achieved more, to have arrived, and so he does what all young men do. He pretends. He plays the role of the person he would like to be but is not yet. He puts on top hat, white tie, and tails and sweeps into the Central Park casino, or sits down with the Round Tablers as if he belongs, or squires a starlet to "21" and signs the tab as if money were no object to him. Gradually he realizes that everyone is playing a role. As he watches the great prepare for social or financial battle, he begins to recognize familiar props, makeup, costumes: Getty with his dyed red hair; Baruch with that scrupulously preserved Southern accent; Billy Rose standing on the grand staircase in his palatial town house playing Lord of the Manor in his forest green smoking jacket. All the world is, indeed, a stage.

Like all actors, I sometimes wonder who I really am. In a life full of changing roles, I look for a center, something constant and enduring. Fortunately, all I need to do is swivel around in my chair and gaze down Park Avenue at the limousines pulling up in front of the sedately Art Deco facade of the Waldorf Astoria or the yellow cabs dodging pedestrians and careening around the balustraded ramps of the old New York Central building toward Park Avenue South.

I have lived in New York all my life — eight decades, going on nine. The better part of a century. This seems, whenever I think about it, remarkable. My brother Bill settled in Connecticut. My brother Albert lives in Los Angeles, my son John in Washington, D.C., my son Philip in Seattle. This is one consequence of our dynamic and mobile economy. The next step in the corporate hierarchy, the tenured academic position, the affordable rents are always to be found somewhere else, so few Americans will die in the place where they were born. But my past still surrounds me in the stones and sidewalks of the city. I see a street sign or the canopy of an apartment building and remember a goodnight kiss or a conversation I had fifty years ago in that very spot.

I fell in love with New York in the thirties. Elegant, sophisticated, tough, witty, skeptical, irreverent, civilized, excessive — it was all these things. That New York may be gone now but I still carry it inside me. Recently, I found myself watching a rerun of Leo McCarey's wonderful 1930s comedy, *The Awful Truth*, with Cary Grant and Irene Dunne. Dunne is on the verge of marrying Ralph Bellamy, a nice but dull oil man from Oklahoma, when she bumps into Grant, her soon-to-be-ex-husband, on one of those vast white sets that stood for a New York nightclub. "So you're going to live in Oklahoma," says Grant, joining them at their table. "Ah, Lucy, how I envy you. Ever since I was a small boy that name has been filled with magic for me ... Oklahoma ... " Taking the bait, Bellamy announces proudly, "We're going to live right in Oklahoma City." Grant arches an eyebrow and deadpans, "Not Oklahoma City itself ... Lucy, you lucky girl." Lucky because, as Grant points out in excruciating detail, she'll have to renounce such frivolous pastimes as prowling around New York shops and nightclub hopping. "I shall think of you every time a new show opens," sighs Grant, "and say to myself, 'She's well out of it.'" Visibly wilting, Dunne attempts the brave rejoinder, "I know I'll enjoy Oklahoma City." "But of course," says Grant politely, "and if it should get dull, you can always go over to Tulsa for the weekend."

I remember when one could expect an audience to share the joke. I remember when New York was the center of the known universe, the object of all desire, and everywhere else was "the sticks." I remember how, for the next twenty years, Hollywood kept recycling that same scene to drive home this point: how in *His Girl Friday*, Grant tries to hold on to ex-wife Rosalind Russell by painting a mockingly glowing picture of what her future life in Albany will be like (with Bellamy again, an insurance man now); how in *Kiss Me Kate* Howard Keel waxes ironic about life in Texas for the benefit of ex-wife Kathryn Grayson on the verge of leaving Broadway forever with a rancher. Times have changed. What used to be thought of as the great nowhere outside of New York City is now looking incredibly sexy in the TV commercials that interrupt these old movies. Desert highway at sunset. Snowy mountainside. A cold beer...Suddenly our dreams seem to be wearing jeans instead of evening clothes. Nor can Oklahoma City ever again be a punch line in a movie now that we will forever link it with that terrible image of a bombed government building.

New York has changed also, of course, mostly for the worse. I can be heard lamenting this at any dinner party. You will never find it listed in those yearly national magazine rankings of the "Ten Best Places to Live." But allow me to repeat a joke I recently heard—in its own muted way, it makes a perfect bookend to the scene in *The Awful Truth*: Ask any New Yorker what he or she thinks of the city and you'll get a litany of complaints. The noise, the street crime, the garbage after a parade, you can't walk in Central Park at night. Ask someone living in Denver and you'll get a blissful smile. Ah, the air, the mountains, Nature, the people are so friendly. Come back in five years and you'll find the New Yorker still grumbling. The Denverite, in the meantime, will have moved on to Seattle (which he or she will praise with the same desperate enthusiasm).

This seems as a good a note to end on as any. I sit at my desk gazing down at a throng of pedestrians hurrying across the street in a light rain, past the grassy center dividers of Park Avenue toward the garden and pool fronting the red and cream stones of St. Bartholomew's Church. The right time, the right place. All that's missing is the sound of Gershwin on the piano, playing for me once again as he did on that memorable early morning so long ago.

In Shakespeare's time, a writer would sometimes close his work with an *envoi*: an address to his own book bidding it to go out into the world and seek its audience. Let me borrow this handy poetic device. Go, little book, part autobiography, part memoir, part corporate history, find your way to some sympathetic and discerning reader and offer him or her this sage counsel. "So long as these pages entertain or instruct, read on. But if, perish the thought, you start to find them dull... well, you can always go to Tulsa for the weekend."

THE END

INDEX

SLINGS AND ARROWS

THEATER IN MY LIFE

by Robert Lewis

"A decidedly good read. Breezy, intelligent, and chatty. A stylish, entertaining, and above all theatrical book."
—The New York Times Book Review

"He's a marvelous storyteller: gossipy, candid without being cruel, and very funny. This vivid, entertaining book is also one of the most penetrating works to be written about the theater."
—Publishers Weekly

"The most interesting book about the theater since Moss Hart's *Act One*."
—Clifton Fadiman

"A superior performance."
—The Los Angeles Times

paper•ISBN 1-55783-244-7

An Actor and His Time

JOHN GIELGUD

"Funny, touching, brilliant, special, the best — exactly like John Gielgud."
—Lauren Bacall

"A wonderful book...the result is magical...Gielgud is the greatest actor of this century...we have no better chronicler of the theatre in his time...an astute observer, a sly humorist."
— Sheridan Morley, *The Literary Review*

"I can hear his superb voice in every line."
— Alec Guinness

"A fascinating account of a legendary career."
— Sunday Telegraph

"A rare delight — full of wit, theatrical history, anecdotes, and wisdom."
— Diana Rigg

cloth • ISBN 1-55783-299-4